PREFACE

In the 1960s young Americans initiated a social revolution that would come to be known as the 'Counterculture.' Parents dubbed it the 'Generation gap' and their children whispered, 'Don't trust anyone over thirty.'

In 1967 the 'Summer of Love' lured 'hippies' from the entire world to San Francisco. In giddy hordes they came with 'flowers in their hair'– smoking pot, dropping acid, listening to psychedelic rock at the Fillmore and cruising Haight-Ashbury and the Castro looking for and finding easy sex.

It was the 'Age of Aquarius' – the time of Woodstock and folk singers – the time of Vietnam and burning draft cards – the time of The Beatles and long hair – the time of Timothy Leary and psychedelic drugs – the time of Andy Warhol and the redefinition of Art.

Traditional mores and values were under attack. Racial segregation was condemned. Discrimination against women and gays was condemned. War was condemned. Materialism was condemned. What a time to be young!

At nineteen I entered another and very different world – the dizzying world of the American super-rich – a peculiar mix of real and bogus aristocracy and frivolous, but feral 'café society.'

In the 1960s those two worlds collided and that collision changed America. The privileged, outdated lifestyle of the super-rich went out of fashion. Their vast estates with scores of servants were too costly to maintain and too difficult to staff. Some of their mansions became museums or clubs, others were subdivided – many were destroyed.

Chapter One

Just a summer job

In 1965 I, unlike the majority of my high school classmates, was not college bound. My parents were unhappy about my (in their opinion) foolish decision. We compromised on a two-year business course at the Collegiate Business Institute in New York City which allowed me a 'student deferment' from the Draft since I was then a full-time student. At the time of the war in Vietnam the menace of the Draft hung over the head of every young American male. Staying in school was the only legal way to avoid it – unless one was incapacitated or the sole surviving son of a father killed in military service. In August 1965 President Lyndon B. Johnson eliminated the marriage exemption from the Draft by an executive order.

However, after one year of studying accounting, I decided that the profession was not for me. Near the end of the school year I wangled an interview with Lee Myers who was in charge of job placement for graduating students of the Institute. Even though she knew I was not returning for the second year, she graciously offered to find me a summer job. A few days later she called me into her cigarette-smoke-fogged office and asked,

"Would you consider taking a domestic job for an individual or a family? I know of several agencies specializing in that field."

I had no idea what she meant, so I asked, "What's a 'domestic job'?"

Mrs. Myers sighed, smiled and explained what was expected from someone engaged in the 'domestic profession' (and trust me, when the job is well done – it *is* a profession.) She said that the so-called 'servant class,' based on the European model so eloquently portrayed in the British miniseries "Upstairs/Downstairs," (and, more recently, "Downton Abbey") was endangered in the United States since upwardly mobile young Americans were not interested in the cloistered, usually boring, dead-end world of 'service.' In other words, despite my shaky draft status, an intelligent young man like I would have *no* problem finding a job in that vanishing profession.

Mrs. Myers explained that because of my age and inexperience I would start in one of the lower male positions. But, she said, I would have no personal expenses – transportation to and from the location, room, board and uniforms would be provided gratis. In 1966 a middle-class male would not ordinarily consider taking a domestic job as a permanent position but I had no such hang-up about a *temporary* summer job. In any case it seemed an offbeat and interesting way to spend my summer.

And, quite honestly, what else could I do – find an uninspiring, low-paying job as a kiddie-pool lifeguard at a country club or an even more boring one – a stock boy in a department store?

So I asked Mrs. Myers to arrange an appointment for me at one of the employment agencies specializing in domestic work. My parents thought me crazy. My maternal Italian grandmother, who considered herself somewhat aristocratic, was embarrassed.

But, to paraphrase Julius Caesar – "The die was cast!"

At that time there were three major agencies in New York City – all on upper Madison Avenue – The Bonfield, The Hedland and The A. E. Johnson. They were all snobbish and stuffy with an abundance of worn brown furniture, dark paintings, and low wattage bulbs burning in lamps with shades askew and, don't forget – no air conditioning! Smoking was universal in 1966 and an acrid cigarette haze permeated all their offices.

Contingent on the kind of work sought, an applicant chose just one agency in which to be 'listed.' It was deemed unwise to be listed at more than one agency at the same time since the agencies frequently shared that information. If one's name was on too many lists it could work against landing a good position.

My first (and only) consultation took place with the owner of the Bonfield agency, Miss MacKay. We hit it off instantly. I told her I just wanted a summer job, but it seemed that Mrs. Myers had already informed her of that – and she said it didn't matter.

My appearance and age, combined with my crazy desire to jump into this new adventure, led to my first job interview.

My potential employer was Mrs. Robert R. Young (née Anita O'Keefe) the widow of New York Central railroad magnate, Robert R. Young. She was traveling through New York on her way from Fairholme, her forty-room summer mansion in Newport, Rhode Island to Montsorrel, her new winter home nearing completion in Palm Beach, Florida.

Anita Ten Eyck O'Keeffe, the middle child of seven children was born 1891. Her father Frank was a simple Wisconsin farmer of Black-Irish ancestry. Ida, her mother, was the daughter of George Victor Totto, a minor Hungarian Count and Isabella Dunham Wyckoff, the daughter of Charles Wyckoff, the scion of a long-established East Coast family of Dutch origin. Unlikely as it seems, the Count's granddaughter and her Irish husband ran a dairy farm in Sun Prairie, Wisconsin.

By the standards of the day the farm was moderately successful. Farm life is difficult and so all the O'Keeffe children had after-school chores – the boys helped with the livestock and the girls cultivated the vegetable garden and were taught to cook and sew. The O'Keeffe's sold their farm in 1902, packed and moved to what they believed to be a healthier location – Williamsburg, Virginia. Anita married Robert Ralph (R.R.) Young in 1916.

Robert, born in 1897 in Canadian, Texas was six years younger than his wife. Rather than work for his banker father, R.R. Young took an unskilled job at the E.I. DuPont gunpowder plant in southern New Jersey. He was a bright young man and was soon promoted to the company treasurer's office where he learned about finance.

In 1922 he joined the General Motors Corporation. He was appointed assistant treasurer in 1928. He predicted the 1929 stock market crash but John J. Raskob the head of General Motors disagreed with him and they parted company. R.R., as we now know, was correct and made his first million by selling stocks short before the crash. He soon started his own brokerage firm and bought a seat on the New York Stock Exchange.

By 1941 he owned controlling interest in the Allegheny Corporation (a railroad holding company) and was the chairman of the board of the Chesapeake and Ohio Railroad.

In 1942 the Youngs bought Fairholme, a handsome Romanesque/shingle-style mansion in Newport. They reputedly paid just 38,000 dollars for it – quite a deal, if true. The house was built for Fairman Rogers, a wealthy sportsman in 1874-75 and was designed by Philadelphia architect Frank Furness, a student of Richard Morris Hunt. Its subsequent owners before the Youngs were the Drexel banking family of Philadelphia and Count and Countess Alphonso P. Villa.

By 1954 R.R. had wrested control of the New York Central Railroad from the Morgans and the Vanderbilts. He was a classic American success story.

Chapter Two

Butlers' Boot Camp

Mrs. Young elected to interview me in her New York apartment rather than visiting the dreary agency and I soon found myself in her penthouse at 900 Fifth Avenue directly across from the Frick Museum.

When the elevator door opened I was greeted by a young parlor-maid who ushered me into a large living room with high ceilings and bright sunlight streaming through its massive windows. The huge paintings hanging on the walls were by Mrs. Young's older sister – Georgia O'Keeffe.

A severe, petite woman in her seventies was seated on the sofa. She had steel gray hair and wore two enormous matching gold bracelets – one on each arm. A tall woman in her mid-forties stood beside her. She was Lorraine, Mrs. Young's Head Cook – a sweet Southern woman who traveled with her more as her companion than her cook.

My interview was for the position of houseman (the entry level for a male) at Fairholme in Newport. It seemed to me at the time that I made a good impression because, after a really brief interview, she hired me. I was immediately informed of the duties I was expected to accomplish each day. The list was written on the back of stationery from 'The Towers,' her mansion in Palm Beach. I still have it. It reads:

Duties: Thomas Gardener

(Please note, my family name is spelled incorrectly)

Breakfast at 7:30 am

1. If necessary, clean and set up fireplaces.

2. Clean both porches outside.

3. Clean brass on both doors every morning.

4. Help with disposal of flowers.

5. Help with dishes in pantry when there are 4 or more people for lunch and help with the dishes in the evening EXCEPT two evenings a week – one when the cook is off and the other when the kitchen maid is off. Those evenings help in kitchen and help's dining room with the dishes.

6. Keep a close check on the windows and see that those, which are dirty, are cleaned without delay.

7. Keep front stairs and back stairs clean.

8. Empty garbage cans at 11 am every day, as well as whenever necessary.

9. Keep flower room clean. Help carry in flower dishes and help with cleaning them.

10. Wax floors in front of the house, first floor, second floor and third floor, back hallways and dining room floor.

11. Be at hand when guests arrive and depart to handle the luggage.

12. Carry laundry baskets upstairs and downstairs.

13. Clean pool dressing rooms after the swimming for the day is finished.

Crazy! An utterly Gargantuan list of *daily* tasks – just reading them now exhausts me.

But I was young and intrigued by Mrs. Young – I'd never met a woman like her. That, coupled with the idea of spending summer in a mansion by the sea, induced me to accept the job.

Back on the street, I telephoned Miss MacKay to tell her the outcome of my interview. She informed me that Mrs. Young had just phoned her and negotiated my salary down because I had no written Reference and therefore she felt it 'fair' to reduce my salary by $25 a week. And I was obliged to pay the agency two weeks salary for the four-month summer job.

"Wow," I thought, "How chintzy can a millionaire be?" It was my first insight into Mrs. Young's personality – but certainly not the last.

Before ending our conversation, Miss MacKay said,

"One more thing Tom. Mrs. Young might ask you to join her for the Winter season in Palm Beach when the summer is over. Whether you go or not is entirely up to you – but if you decide not to, be sure to get a written Reference signed by Mrs. Young herself."

"Why?" I asked.

"If you decide, for whatever reason, to seek work in this profession again, signed written References are absolute necessities. Lacking them, your prospective employer will assume you did not perform the work satisfactorily at your previous job and will not hire you," she replied.

"I will do that Miss MacKay. Thank you," I said and thought, "Why does she think I might want to make this my life's work? She knows it's just a summer job."

On the following Monday afternoon I arrived in Newport on a Greyhound bus. Joe, Mrs. Young's head gardener met me at the bus station in his classic 1950s Ford pick-up truck and we drove to Fairholme.

Joe was a jovial Portuguese man descended from Newport's first fishermen settlers. At estates like Fairholme with circumscribed grounds, gardeners like Joe generally lived in their own homes.

Joe decided to enter the property by the semicircular front drive. He said that since Mrs. Young was still in Palm Beach she wouldn't know. As we drove up to the house he motioned to the perfectly groomed lawn and said,

"Just look at that lawn Tom – it's the most beautiful lawn in Newport – Mrs. Young insists that everything here must be absolutely perfect."

Then he related an amusing story about Fairholme's address. The name of the street where Fairholme is located is Ruggles Avenue. For one reason or another, Mrs. Young hated that name. Since 'The Breakers' (the Vanderbilt 'cottage') is located across the street, Mrs. Young preferred to refer to Fairholme as being located on the same street as the celebrated mansion – Ochre Point Avenue.

As we approached the house, garrulous Joe leaned over to me and whispered that if I found any actions by Mrs. Young's Butler, Valdemar unusual or strange, I should tell him immediately. I wasn't quite sure just what he was referring to – but I would soon find out.

We entered by the service entrance. I suppose Joe didn't dare use the front door when the in-house staff was around to notice. Then I was introduced to them one by one.

The first was Louise, a middle-aged American woman who was the parlor-maid/waitress, the second was a young French girl named Jeanne who was the kitchen aid and acted as second cook when Lorraine was away. Next came Manny the chauffeur, a handsome, well-built, six-foot-four German American somewhere in his late thirties.

And last, but most certainly not least was Flora, Mrs. Young's personal lady's maid. Flora was a bitter 'old maid,' shorter than Mrs. Young and older by several years. She reminded me of one of those Pennsylvania Dutch dolls whose heads are made of shriveled-up apples. Flora had been with Mrs. Young for a very long time.

Two people were absent from my staff introduction. The first was Lorraine, the Head Cook, who I had already met in New York at the interview and would not see until she and Mrs. Young returned from Florida.

The last was the notorious Polish Butler – Valdemar, who arrived ten minutes later. Joe's warning (to take care when dealing with him) now took on some weight. Valdemar was in his mid-fifties, tall and lean, with salt and pepper hair and dark, deep-set eyes. His skin had a yellow pallor. He reminded me of Bela Lugosi as Dracula. He spoke English with a peculiar European accent. He, like Flora had been with Mrs. Young for many years.

He seemed a bit over-dramatic and initially gave me an uneasy feeling. That aside, he taught me the ins and outs of the workings of Fairholme in short order and in the end turned out to be a rather decent fellow. He instructed me that Mrs. Young must never be called anything other than 'Madam.' And he said that staff was never, under any circumstances, permitted to use the guests' 'Powder Room' located near the front door.

Oh yes, there was one other member of the staff – Madam's Social Secretary Miss Coffin. Miss Coffin was an imposing spinster in her late fifties with the charm of a Marine Drill Sargent. She endlessly alluded to her father having been an executive at the Hewlett-Packard Corporation in an effort to elevate her 'position' to more than it actually was – as if anyone cared.

Her office and apartment were on the second floor of the old carriage house that functioned as Madam's garage for her two cars. It was a massive structure with arched Richardsonian doors and had once accommodated horse-drawn carriages.

Madam owned a grey 1958 Rolls-Royce Silver Wraith limousine. The other vehicle was a 1957 blue and white, four-door Ford Fairlane that had been the late Mr. Young's personal car. Manny the chauffeur kept them both in impeccable condition.

Staff quarters when viewed from Cliff Walk were in the right wing of the house. The first floor contained the kitchen, the Butler's pantry, the laundry room complex and the staff dining room where buffet-style breakfasts, lunches and dinners were provided. The second and third floors held the staff dormitories. Women were billeted on the second floor – men on the third.

When Fairholme was built the term 'servant's quarters' was well chosen. The staff rooms were small, just ten by twelve feet with a bed, a small chest of draws, a small closet and a simple reading chair with a nearby floor lamp. Bath and toilet facilities were communal. The best thing about my room was its dormer window which opened to the great lawn and the Ocean beyond.

Fairholme was, as were most nineteenth-century mansion houses, built of two interlocking sections – the so-called 'front' of the house where the family lived and the 'back' where the staff lived and worked. Access from 'back' to 'front' was limited. On the upper two floors access was through a single corridor door. On the main floor there were two accesses – the first was through a narrow hall that led to the entrance hall – the second led from the Butler's pantry to the formal dining room.

The first floor of the 'back' of the house held no staff facilities. When nature called one was obliged to climb up the back staircase to the second or third floor, walk down a long corridor and when finished, reverse the process. If someone else was using the facility when one arrived – one waited.

As late as the 1960s the live-in staff of upper class families considered themselves servants. They were not ambitious, often coming from families that had been 'in service' for generations. They were frequently so servile that I began to regard them as 'professional lackeys.' In general, their age range was mid- to late-forties – but some were much older. They were invariably white Christians, lacking high school diplomas. They regarded their positions as permanent and had no desire to advance. In other words – a houseman would *never* aspire to rise to the level of Butler.

Madam's maid Flora immediately sensed that I was not one of them. On rare occasions when our paths crossed she'd simply stare at me with her beady eyes, mumble something unintelligible (undoubtedly a comment on her dismay at my very existence) and continue on. I regarded her as my personal Madame Defarge – *sans* knitting needles.

Madam and Lorraine returned from Palm Beach several days after my arrival. And soon the weekend guests began to arrive – the first were two impressive Grandes Dames. Before my time her guests had included the duke and duchess of Windsor, her Newport neighbor Rose Kennedy and her son John and his wife, Jackie. I was told the president often swam in Fairholme's heated pool to ease his back pain.

One of the Grandes Dames that arrived that day was 'Tucky' Guest. Her arrival will always remain one of my favorite memories of that summer.

When I looked up from my assigned task I saw a vision driving through the front gate of Fairholme. Set against the lawn's superb, manicured green expanse, I saw a long, fire engine red Chrysler 300 convertible approaching – the lady herself at the wheel. That alone impressed me. Then a most beautiful woman alighted, smiled graciously, and asked,

"Would you please see to it that the tank is filled?"

"Certainly," I replied, enraptured.

Although there was an actual functioning gas pump on the property, I was instructed to drive into town in order to 'tank-up' Mrs. Guest's car. I often wonder if she was presented a bill for the gas? Knowing Madam, that wasn't out of the question.

The weekend progressed briskly – breakfasts, luncheons, pool parties, cocktail and dinner parties followed seamlessly one upon the another.

Valdemar performed his Buttling duties beautifully – each and every detail was orchestrated. While I never directly assisted him in serving a meal – the parlor-maid/waitress Louise did, I did help in the Butler's pantry with all the items coming out of the kitchen and I was in charge of the washing-up. The countless stages required to serve a simple three-course meal amazed me.

Madam and her guests were of course, on a first or nickname basis. These nicknames, some bordering on the ridiculous, were all but universal in their social circle. On several occasions, I overheard Mrs. Young and her friends refer to or address Mrs. Guest as 'Tucky.'

I didn't know that an unwritten rule existed – these silly nicknames were *never, under any circumstances* to be used by staff members. So, at one staff luncheon I, in all innocence, made the unforgivable blunder of referring to Mrs. Guest as 'Tucky.'

Flora glared at me as if I had uttered some filthy, four-letter word. Her hostility to me was so obvious that I felt I would soon have problems with her. In time my impression was proven true.

Madam was an obsessive perfectionist. For instance, there were luxurious, pale beige, silk-blend carpets in the reception room, library and living room. They revealed every footprint. So, every morning before ten they had to be 'combed' back to perfection. The chore was performed with the use of two tools – each made from the shaft and brush of an Electrolux vacuum cleaner. Imagine this – Louise and I progressing slowly backwards in tandem and erasing the footprints of the previous day's social activities.

As Madam entertained infrequently, there should have been no need to perform this footprint ballet daily. But one morning I saw her striding through each room, creating with childlike glee a trail of footprints which would have to be erased later that day by her two 'carpet combers.' Her behavior seemed to me at once baffling and somewhat cruel.

She wasn't evil. Her firm control of her daily life (specifically when dealing with the staff) was perhaps an understandable reaction to life's tragedies that had befallen her – tragedies over which she had had no control.

Her only child Eleanor was killed in a private plane crash near Newport in 1941. 'Cookie' (as her friends nicknamed her) was one of the 'Glamour Girls' of the 1930's and her 1936 debut was among the most lavish celebrations in Newport history.

Flouting her parents' wishes in 1939, Eleanor married Robert Ogden (Bunty) Bacon Jr., a handsome society playboy. They divorced eight months later. Her accidental death was a great shock to the Youngs.

In January 1958, despondent from business reversals and never having fully recovered from the death of his daughter, Robert Young took his life with a shotgun in the billiard room of 'The Towers,' the couple's Palm Beach mansion.

Madam's sister Georgia O'Keeffe came down to help her deal with her second tragedy.

Sans daughter and husband, Madam spent the rest of her life requiring control and perfection in every aspect of her world.

One morning as I was carrying a vase of faded flowers from the entrance hall, I heard a loud, enraged male voice coming from inside the library. I cautiously glanced inside. It was Valdemar and the target of his rage was – Madam herself.

"I won't stay in this house another minute!" he roared. "I'm leaving now! I'm going back to Poland where a person of my quality and background is truly appreciated." Then he stormed out of the room.

I almost dropped the vase when I saw Madam staring at me with a look that could have turned me to stone. She was obviously mortified that I overheard the extraordinary confrontation.

So I went back to the pantry and held my breath. After several minutes passed and Madam did not appear, I resumed my duties.

When I had finished my morning chores Valdemar called me on the house phone and asked if I would help him pack. When I knocked and entered his room he was sitting on the edge of his bed. I noticed that his bags had already been packed. As it turned out, he just wanted to vent.

"That old woman is a witch. In my country," he said standing up and wagging his index finger at me, "people like her would be working for me. She spends all her time thinking of ways to torture me. She's a lowborn peasant! She grew up milking cows on a farm. It's no wonder that everyone here calls her 'Anita, the parlor-maid' behind her back!"

I actually never heard anyone in the house use that particular sobriquet when referring to the venerable Madam.

Valdemar was gone the next morning. After staff breakfast Miss Coffin called me to her office and told me that Madam decided to elevate me to the position of her 'Butler-in-Training.' Some of my houseman 'duties' like rug-combing would be reassigned to one of the female staff. The more laborious tasks however, remained mine.

And by the way, there would be no raise in salary – not even the restoration of the twenty-five dollars a week Mrs. Young had seen fit to deduct from my original contract. Actually, it was fine with me. It was worth twenty-five dollars a week not to have to 'comb' those disgusting rugs each and every day.

On large estates the Steward is in charge of the entire house and grounds. Under him the positions of Butler, footman (aka Under Butler,) valet, chauffeur and houseman are reserved for men. If there is no Steward, the top male staff member is the Butler and descends to the humble houseman. The top woman is the Housekeeper seconded by the Head Cook and so on down the line to the kitchen aids, parlor- or personal (lady's)-maids and laundresses. The staff's pay scale is determined by position, not seniority.

Most estates today are not large enough for a Steward so the always-male Butler and his female counterpart, the Housekeeper, with more or less equal authority, are in charge of the rest of the staff. They are the only staff members having direct contact with the family.

The Butler deals directly with the male staff of one or more Under-Butlers, the valet, the chauffeur and one or more housemen. His primary task however, is supervising food services. He is responsible for all the table settings, including the placement of the linens, china, silver, flower arrangements and candelabra.

To facilitate this the 'Butler's pantry' is kept fully stocked and meticulously organized. In most big houses it is a large room situated between the kitchen and the formal dining room. It is used to store numerous sets of china, crystal and silver that are needed for the various functions. The china and crystal are usually kept in tall, glass-front cabinets for easy viewing, the linens (tablecloths, doilies for under the fingerbowls, breakfast tray linens, napkins, etc.) are kept in drawers underneath.

The sterling silver flatware and large serving pieces (candelabra, soup tureens, platters, etc.) are usually kept in a large, walk-in, combination safe. All the silver is kept scrupulously clean and polished.

Under the Housekeeper is the Head Cook who is in charge of the kitchen aids. Next comes an assortment of maids – starting with the parlor-maids who frequently double as waitresses who help the Butler with the meal services, followed by a personal lady's maid and lastly the lowly laundresses who were day help and rarely lived-in.

The task of greeting guests at the door, a popular misconception of a Butler's job, usually falls to one of the Under-Butlers.

I soon discovered that there are very few homes in this country with a large enough staff to qualify anyone to hold the traditional title of 'Butler.' As you will see, in most of my positions I was either – the Butler/chauffeur, the Butler/man-Friday or the Butler/valet. Only at one point in my career did I attain the level of the traditional, Hollywood-style Butler. That was when I was employed by Dr. and Mrs. Leon Levy who maintained a staff of nine for just the two of them and lived a quiet life. They rarely entertained and *never* had house guests – not even family.

As Madam's 'Butler-in-Training,' I was required to wear traditional Butler's Livery. So, later that morning Louise and I climbed to the third floor of the staff wing and looked through several walk-in closets filled with old uniforms used by former staff members.

It seems that Mrs. Young disposed of nothing that was in possibly re-useable condition – probably a holdover from her thrifty childhood. We found numerous Butler's uniforms including one that once belonged to Valdemar. But it took half an hour to find one that actually fit me.

I was scheduled to meet with Madam at two that afternoon in the Butler's pantry to begin my 'Training.' And my tutor in the 'Art of Buttling' was to be Madam herself.

She decided that during my course of instruction, it would be best if I did everything alone – that is, without the help of Louise, the parlor-maid/waitress who normally assisted Valdemar in serving. The stage was now set for what was to be an enlightening experience – one which would serve me well in the years to come.

My classroom was to be Fairholme's eight-hundred-square-foot dining room. The table was twelve feet long and, depending on how many leaves were inserted, could seat eighteen. The bay window niche, with its ocean view over Cliff Walk held a breakfast or luncheon table seating six.

Madam usually dined alone and insisted two more place settings be set to her immediate left and right. Her invisible guests (her late husband and daughter?) never appeared.

For some unknown reason she positioned her chair at the farthest point from the pantry door. This necessitated the Butler and the parlor-maid/waitress to traverse the entire length of the room twice for the serving of each and every course.

Madam was a strict taskmaster and under her tutelage I soon became a qualified Butler.

She taught me to:

1. Set a table for a formal dinner party with the linens, china, crystal and silver she had selected.

2. Both choose and assemble all the serving equipment that would be required for the luncheon or dinner.

3. Be capable of both serving and supervising the event from start to finish.

4. NEVER to be bullied by older staff members, especially when dealing with events directly under my supervision.

5. NEVER to be intimidated by the names or titles of those you were serving.

A formal Dinner for one

Madam's daily dinner ritual began when Lorraine, the Head Cook informed me that the kitchen was ready. Dressed in my second-hand Butler's livery I ascended the Grand Staircase to her second-floor bedroom suite. I knocked softly on the closed door and said, "Madam, dinner is served." Back downstairs I stood by the door to the dining room and waited for Madam's arrival. When she appeared, I escorted her to the head of the table and held her chair as she sat.

When she was seated I went back to the pantry to fetch her tiny bowl of soup (it was always soup, usually a cold consommé) and the ritual began. I entered the dining room and again walked its entire length and set the soup before her on her place plate. Then I went back to the pantry for two pieces of Melba toast wrapped in a folded linen napkin placed on a small sterling silver tray. Back and forth again!

A sterling-silver Georgian bell was always set on the table before her. When she finished the soup she rang it to signal she was ready for the next course and I returned with a warmed dinner plate. Then I adeptly lifted the place plate and the empty soup bowl with one white-gloved hand and placed the dinner plate in front of Madam with the other – a ballet move to be proud of.

Then back to the pantry for the main course which usually consisted of meat and vegetables, offered separately. So after I served the meat I walked back to the pantry for the vegetables. And then another trip for two warm dinner rolls. And then an encore for a second offering of the main course. Back and forth, and back and forth, again and again!

When Madam finished she rang her bell to inform me to come back and remove the dinner plate, the bread and butter plate, the salt and pepper shakers and finally 'crumb' the table. Then I set her desert service, which had been placed on the nearby sideboard before her.

Dessert, cookies and coffee were three separate offerings, each requiring the usual back and forth from the dining room to the pantry and back.

(When she dined alone she skipped the traditional formal-dinner cheese course. In a standard formal dinner the coffee service was served in the library with after-dinner liquors and candies.)

Ten endless days later, when Madam felt I had mastered her formal dining ritual she allowed Louise to resume her duties as the parlor-maid waitress and assist me as she had Valdemar.

Madam dined slowly. Lorraine, Louise and I waited endlessly in the Butler's pantry for the sound of the bell. Lorraine loved dancing and decided to teach me to tango on those interminable intermissions. She hummed a tune and we tangoed away while an amused Louise looked on. One evening as we waited an unusually long time for the ringing of Madam's bell, I thought,

"What the hell is she doing with those four spoonsful of soup?"

A moment later the swinging door connecting the pantry to the dining room crashed into the pantry wall rattling all the china and crystal. Madam, furious and clutching her bell, strode across the room and approached me. Thrusting the bell at me, she said,

"Here dummy, take this! And remember, the next time you decide to polish my dinner bell, be so kind as to replace the clapper!"

Having made her point, she turned on a dime and went back to the dining room. I glanced at the counter where I had spent all afternoon polishing the silver for the evening meal and low and behold, there lay the clapper. So I quickly reunited bell with clapper, placed it on a sterling silver tray and carried it back to the dining room with aplomb. I approached Madam, offered the bell to her and was rewarded as she looked up and smiled at me for the very first time.

Madam's dining room table held two large sterling silver candelabra and the breakfast table in the niche held one. There were several candlesticks on the mantle illuminating a huge Georgia O'Keeffe painting. Madam kept examples of her sister's work in her three homes.

Even when dining alone, Madam insisted that *all* the candles burn during the dinner service. However, she left the windows slightly ajar in order to capture the ocean breezes off Cliff Walk. Therefore, by the end of any given evening meal, there were melted candle drippings (aka 'angel fluff') on the candelabra, the table and all the other surfaces where the hot flying wax could land. This guaranteed hours of intensive cleaning (by me) the next morning.

I found the entire performance ludicrous inasmuch as Valdemar had recently informed me of Madam's less-than-aristocratic origins. And her dining ritual (she had breakfast brought up to her room and usually took lunch by the pool) was so theatrical that I actually felt I was onstage in an outlandish, bizarre play – well, perhaps I was.

Madam was not socially active. When it came to Newport's bustling summer schedule, she preferred to host an occasional, formal dinner party for six or eight.

Alternatively she chose to entertain guests at her magnificent pool pavilion. The pavilion, of a beautiful contemporary design cost 250,000 dollars to build in 1958 the year her husband died. It was in great contrast to the elegance of Fairholme, yet somehow didn't look out of place. One of the pavilion's four walls consisted of huge sliding glass doors that, with the push of a button, opened to the waters of the Atlantic. Madam spent an hour each day at the heated pool where she routinely swam countless laps to keep in shape.

During the hot summer months Madam frequently flew to Palm Beach to supervise the latest phase of the construction of Montsorrel, her new mansion on North County Road. When finished

Montsorrel, named for some indefinite reason after a village in Leicestershire, England would be the second largest home in Palm Beach after Marjorie Post's Mar-a-Lago.

Madam's cook/companion Lorraine enjoyed accompanying Madam to Palm Beach out of season since she could stay in her cozy Spanish-style house in West Palm Beach where she and her husband Danny spent the Winter season. In the Summer season he was the chauffeur for Dr. and Mrs. Leon Levy in Philadelphia while Lorraine worked at Fairholme.

Madam was such a compulsive perfectionist apropos the construction of her new mansion that it was rumored she drove the contractors mad. Household scuttlebutt maintained that one of them committed suicide due to her extreme perfectionism – it seemed that a small window over the main entrance was an inch and a half off-center.

The origin of Montsorrel is a sad tale.

In 1946 the Youngs bought the former Winter home of the millionaire radio manufacturer Arthur Atwater Kent for a reputed 160,000 dollars. It was called 'The Towers.' It was a typical Palm Beach, Spanish-style pastiche – and a good deal smaller than Fairholme.

The Youngs attempted to enter Palm Beach society but were not successful. They were considered 'new money' and were therefore not qualified to mingle with those who believed themselves to be that perfect oxymoron, 'American Aristocracy.'

They countered with a brilliant ploy.

Mr. Young met the duke of Windsor at a business luncheon in New York in May 1943 and invited him and the duchess to Fairholme, his recently-acquired Newport mansion. The Windsors accepted his invitation and the couples soon became good and lasting friends. So, when the Palm Beach set snubbed them, the Youngs invited the duke and duchess to sojourn at 'The Towers' for part of the Winter season. When the ex-British King and his spouse appeared in Palm Beach, the Youngs instantly achieved the social acceptance they desired.

In January 1958 Robert Young took his own life with a shotgun in the billiard room of 'The Towers.' The year before I began work at Fairholme, Madam decided to raze 'The Towers' and build a new mansion 'Montsorrel' on the same footprint. It always seemed strange to me that she didn't simply sell it and buy or build a new mansion somewhere else.

I quickly became proficient at supervising and/or serving formal dinner parties for six to eight guests. At each dinner's conclusion, Madam and her guests would withdraw to the library for coffee, after-dinner liquors and candies. There Madam would offer a selection of chocolates on a silver tray. These special bonbons were not kept in the Butler's pantry as they would have been in any other mansion but upstairs in Madam's dressing room under lock and key.

Madam's personal maid, my nemesis Flora was charged with delivering an allotted number of these transcendent chocolates to the library and the return of those that had not been eaten to Madam's dressing room after the guests had departed.

One evening dinner went really well and the guests had left by midnight. Louise, Lorraine and I squared away the library and had finished closing down the pantry when Flora appeared and announced she was there to escort the uneaten chocolates back to Madam's dressing room lock-box.

The next morning Flora entered the staff dining room in full Gestapo mode. You see Madam had counted the precise number of chocolates that remained on the tray after the guests departed and concluded that one was missing!

Madam demanded to know who had eaten it and sent Flora downstairs to act the Grand Inquisitor. No one admitted to the heinous crime but I was of the opinion that it was Flora herself that gobbled up the chocolate on her way up to Madam's dressing room.

So at all staff meals for the next several days, Flora steered the conversation to the same subject. "Who could have eaten that piece of chocolate?" she asked rhetorically and glowered at me.

Flower arranging was Madam's hobby for many years. So my favorite duty as 'Butler-in-Training' was assisting her arrange a dozen or so fresh floral displays to be placed throughout the mansion. The flowers (and a good deal of fruits and vegetables) came from "The Farm." Madam owned a farm in Fall River, Massachusetts where a large staff of farm workers cared for the fruit trees, the vegetable gardens and flowerbeds.

Every day Joe in his pick-up would enter the drive at Fairholme, stop at the flower room to drop off five or six pails of flowers before proceeding to the back door of the kitchen to deliver the freshly-picked fruits and vegetables.

Madam built her flower room at the far end of the never-used ballroom. Since the ballroom was located at the extreme end of the main floor and the flower room projected even further out towards the pool pavilion, it was accessible from the front drive. So, the numerous pails of fresh flowers could arrive without having to pass through the main rooms of the front of the house.

I realized that I looked forward to the afternoon flower-arranging hours I spent with Madam. She enjoyed doing the arrangements and seemed to relax. When the two of us were alone and far from the other staff, it was not unusual for Madam to comment, "Well done Thomas."

She loved Steuben crystal and used their very heavy vases for all our flower arrangements. One day we created three huge arrangements. When we finished Madam turned to me and said,

"Thomas, put the tallest arrangement in the large reception room and don't forget to fill it with water."

Not wanting to set the ponderous object down in the wrong room and then move it again, I asked,

"Excuse me Madam, but which room is the large reception room?" This time she actually laughed out loud, and said,

"Thomas the large reception room is bigger than the small reception room."

Now why didn't I think of that?

Just off the Great Hall was the guests' 'Powder Room' that Valdemar warned me of on my first day. Except for its daily cleaning this 'room' was strictly off limits to the staff.

Of course, I used it whenever I needed to. Why bother to climb the stairs to the third-floor men's communal toilet when I didn't have to?

In order to accomplish that risky undertaking, I'd first determine where the other staff members and Madam might be. Then, assured of my safety, I would enter the forbidden place for a quick 'visit.' It became a game for me. The more I did it, the bolder I became.

One morning when I had finished laying out all items needed for Madam's luncheon with two guests, the urge arose and I threw caution to the winds and dashed off to the Powder Room without checking everyone's location.

Mid-stream, I sensed a presence outside the door.

"THOMAS?" asked Madam herself.

I realize now the impact that a single word can carry. I can only compare it to what it must have been like hearing the word 'ICEBERG!' on the Titanic. I lifted the scrub brush and opened the door. I wanted to appear to be making a final spot-check prior to the arrival of the luncheon guests.

I thought I fooled her. What was I thinking? I was little David against a female Goliath! As we walked in tandem to the dining room for the final check, Madam, without even looking at me – said five words,

"Thomas, your fly is open!" and added,

"Don't let Flora catch you doing that again – there'd be hell to pay."

I never used the Powder Room again. Because of this incident and despite her idiosyncrasies, I was honestly beginning to like Madam.

At nineteen my beard's color and growth was still rather light and I normally didn't need to shave every day. One morning as I was working somewhere in the front of the house I came face to face with Madam while standing near a window with the morning sun streaming through.

She looked at me and asked,

"Thomas, did you shave today?"

I hadn't but in a panic, I said I had. Madam with her dry Midwestern sense of humor replied, "Thomas, stand closer to the blade the next time you shave."

Against all odds, Madam and I were getting on rather well. She was an intelligent and perceptive woman and I believe she understood that I was not at all like the other members of her staff.

One afternoon as we were arranging flowers, I felt the moment had arrived when I could ask her for something I had been considering for a while. I asked her if it might be possible, once my daily duties had been completed, for me to use the Ford Fairlane once a week in the evening.

Remember, it was her late husband's personal car and no one had ever been permitted to use it. Without hesitation and to my great surprise she said, "Yes."

I mentioned Madam's unexpected generosity at staff dinner that night and told them I was planning to go into town soon to experience Newport's night life, Manny and Flora were fit to be tied. Manny angrily stated to all present,

"I can't believe it. I take care of that car as if it was my own – why should *he* be able to use it." Flora just sat and stared at me with daggers in her eyes.

One evening a week or so later when I arrived back at Fairholme I found the garage door locked. It was only about ten-fifteen but there were no lights in either the staff wing or in Miss Coffin's apartment above the garage.

I didn't want to wake anyone so, locking the car and taking the keys with me, I left the Ford outside on the drive. Waking up early the next morning, I dashed out to deal with the garage door issue and what did I see?

Manny was hosing down the car to remove the salt sea spray that had coated it overnight and, with a satiric grin, said,

"Madam's not going to think too kindly of the car staying out all night."

I told him that *someone* had purposely locked the garage door and that I would tell Madam exactly that if she decided to rescind my permission to use the car. He evidently decided not to say anything for the subject of the locked garage door never came up.

I was well aware that most of the staff members disliked me. I had crossed that sacrosanct line between master and servant – an act they could neither understand nor accept – and my free spirit frightened them.

In mid-August Madam and Lorraine flew to Palm Beach to oversee the progress at Montsorrel. Madam was obsessed with finishing every detail to allow the duke and duchess to spend the upcoming Winter season in their sumptuous new quarters – quarters that she had especially designed for them.

For a reason known but to her, she had become one of the notorious couple's so-called ladies-in-waiting, hosting them in Palm Beach every Winter season. She had even recreated the British Royal Crest over the entrance to their new suite at Montsorrel.

Madam and Lorraine planned to stay away for several days. Although there were no houseguests during her absence, the pool pavilion was well used. Madam had granted permission to several of her Newport lady friends to use the pool while she was away.

Three to five ladies arrived at poolside at eleven each morning. I recognized several of them as having been Madam's recent luncheon or dinner guests.

They expected to be treated as if they were goddesses descended from Mount Olympus. I supplied them with piles of luxurious, oversized towels, suntan lotions, lemonade and other soft drinks and a lunch buffet of sandwiches and fresh fruit. I reappeared frequently to tidy up and replenish whatever was needed.

Because of my duties, I overheard their unguarded conversations. One must understand that these sixtyish, to-the-manner-born society ladies, regarded me as they did the servants they had grown up with – an invisible, mute, eunuch.

Consequently they said anything they liked, secure in the fact that I would never absorb or dare to repeat anything I heard them say. So there in the pool pavilion that day's three harridans lounged, enjoying the food and drink Madam generously provided and all the while – maligning her.

They found no end of amusement ridiculing Madam's 'airs' when it came to hosting the duke and duchess of Windsor. The fact that she addressed the duke as "Sir" and the duchess as "Your Royal Highness" even though British 'letters patent' banned her from using that title, engendered gales of laughter.

They mocked her curtsy to the duke when he attended functions at Fairholme. And they found it ridiculous that she seated the duke and duchess at the opposite ends of her dinner table and had them served first, as if they were the owners of Fairholme, not she.

One said the duchess was really a man not a woman. A second retorted, "No dear, I've heard that she's a hermaphrodite."

The third asked, "What's that?"

"Half-man, half-woman," glibly answered the second while munching on a sandwich.

"Do you think Anita pays them to stay here?" asked the first, "Everyone says they have no money and freeload all over the world."

"We'll never know," answered the third, "but it's just the kind of thing Anita would do. You know she grew up on a farm in Wisconsin of all places, and that she slept four to a bed with her sisters."

"Anita thinks that money makes her one of us," declared the second.

"Can you imagine!" sneered the other two, almost in unison.

They continued to degrade Madam, whose origins, in their eyes, was from a class well below their own. They joked about her 'folly' of rebuilding her Palm Beach mansion in on such a grand scale. They wondered if she would hang her sister Georgia's 'dreadful' paintings in it.

They went on all afternoon. I was appalled and angry at their callousness.

To this day I'm not certain just why their malicious gossip was so offensive to me. Perhaps it was because I was an idealistic nineteen-year old or maybe it was my non-judgmental upbringing or it could have been my frustration in not being able to voice my own objections to those three parasites.

But I decided that there was only one acceptable remedy. On her return from Florida, I would tell Madam exactly what they said about her. My only remaining question was – how?

After reviewing all methods open to me I decided that a personal note in my own hand would best accomplish my goal. In retrospect, perhaps it wasn't the most judicious choice. However, at that moment my inner Don Quixote would not be silenced – I too was a noble knight defending a lady in distress.

Putting pen to paper in the privacy of my room, I clearly stated how vicious Madam's lady friends had been behind her back and at her pool, no less. I chose to leave my note in an unsealed envelope on her dressing table before she returned. It never occurred to me that Flora would read the note and inform Miss Coffin of its content immediately.

At breakfast the following morning a smirking Flora informed me,

"I want you to know that Valdemar is back and Miss Coffin wants to see you right now."

I stopped eating and walked to Miss Coffin's office. On my way I thought,

"What's this all about. I thought he was gone forever."

I arrived at her office in the carriage house, walked up the stairs and knocked. She was sitting at her desk, haughty as always. She motioned me to sit down and said,

"Thomas, Valdemar has returned to Fairholme and is going to resume his position today. You will return to your duties as houseman immediately. Thank you, you may leave." Short, pompous – and icy cold.

Well, I had no intention of resuming that tedious and boring routine – visions of combing rugs flashed before my eyes. I had, thanks to Madam's training, become an accomplished Butler and Manny, on Madam's instructions, had instructed me on the 'ins and outs' of chauffeuring the Rolls. The fact that my transition had taken place in such a short time was, in hindsight, amazing. All in all, a great deal of learning had taken place during Valdemar's absence.

So, I countered, "I'd like to speak to Mrs. Young."

She retorted instantly and angrily, "Mrs. Young will not wish to speak to you when she returns," and turned away.

"She *will* speak to me," I said.

With an icy stare she retorted,

"Thomas, this conversation is over, I wish to hear no further comments from you. Go back to the house. Flora will give you your instructions."

I returned to the house confused, upset and unsure of what to do and went directly to my room. I was certainly not going to submit myself to Flora's whims. Her revenge would be swift. She'd order me to scrub all the staff toilets – or something equally disgusting.

I remembered Joe, the head gardener's warning regarding Valdemar when I first arrived and so I decided to speak to him. I waited for him in the flower room.

Later that morning he arrived with that day's supply of flowers. (Louise and I did the arrangements in Madam's absence.) He was pleased to see me and quickly noticed that I was upset.

"What's wrong Tom?" he asked.

"Valdemar is back and Miss Coffin ordered me to resume to my houseman duties. What happened?"

"Oh my," he said, "I thought you knew the whole story by now."

"What story?"

"Every two years or so Valdemar goes a little crazy and quits in the middle of the Summer season. He always comes back in time for the closing of Fairholme and the move to Palm Beach in October. This time he's back a few weeks ahead of schedule."

"Really?" was all I could say.

"This is the way it goes. When he returns he apologizes to Madam for 'blowing-up' and leaving. She tells him how good he has it here and she takes him back. They're like a married couple – they fight, they make up, they fight again. It's been going on for years. Lorraine told me when Madam first met you at your interview in New York she realized that you'd be perfect in the event that Valdemar had another one of his 'blow-ups.' He was already acting moody so I guess she was hedging her bets.

Madam told Lorraine that you were nice looking and smart and thought you could easily be his replacement for the summer, if the situation arose. I'm sorry you didn't know."

Indeed, I did *not* know and I felt manipulated and angry. To coin a phrase, "My Irish was up!" So, after my conversation with Joe I went straight to Coffin's office. I knocked and walked in without waiting for her invitation. She seemed startled.

"Why didn't anyone here tell me my position as Butler was temporary – just a waiting game until Valdemar reappeared?"

She didn't answer my question, but said,

"Thomas, I think it best that you leave Fairholme now. Flora told me that you've been much too familiar with Madam. Flora says she's seen you laughing and joking with Madam on several occasions and Manny told me that you prevailed upon her to let you use her husband's car. You don't know your place. And regarding the letter you left on Madam's dressing table – it's beyond belief. You forget young man that you are a *servant* here."

She took a deep breath and went on, "It's *my* duty to protect Madam from presumptuous people like you. I'll call Greyhound and make a reservation for you on the four o'clock bus to New York. Joe will pick you up at three. Go pack your things. Come back here in an hour and I'll have your check ready."

"Fine," I said, then turned and left her office.

When I came back for my check she handed it to me and said,

"I spoke to Madam in Florida and we decided that since you are leaving under questionable circumstances we both feel it would neither be proper nor appropriate to give you a Reference."

She was lying. I knew it. I'm sure she told Mrs. Young that I quit. On the Greyhound back to New York I reflected on the numerous events of that incredible summer.

It was the summer I learned how to iron my own shirts and trousers. It was the summer I learned how to care for antique silver and valuable china. It was the summer I learned the art of floral display. It was the summer I was away from my family for the first time and learned to be self-sufficient. And it was the summer I learned how to be a Butler.

When I returned to New York I moved back home with my parents.

Often, in the darkening evening when we sat down to dinner, I thought of Mrs. Young –
dining alone with her dripping candles ablaze – Valdemar hovering in the background – and
those empty place settings on either side of her and I felt sad – and very lucky.

I wrote a second letter and thanked her for the transformational days I spent at Fairholme. I
made no mention of her gossiping friends.

She didn't reply.

Chapter Three

Suzanne (Suzy) Gardner

The Name Game

In early September I began looking for a job in New York City. But a twenty-year old with
no experience and no college degree had virtually no chance of finding a job with a future which
is what I wanted – I had had enough of futureless, dead-end domestic work. In addition my draft
status had not changed and no one wanted to hire someone who could be whisked off to war at
any moment.

After several weeks in my parents' home, fruitlessly pouring through countless job listings of
the usual nine-to-five 'Executive Trainee' programs and several fruitless interviews, I thought,

"To hell with this!" and decided to visit the A.E. Johnson agency to see what was available.
(I had heard good things about their list of top-notch clients.)

The owner, Miss Olivia herself met with me and after a long discussion of my summer at
Fairholme, immediately arranged several interviews for me. Thanks to Mrs. Young's training,

my profile became that of a 'Junior-Butler.' My new title was an honest and fair evaluation of my capabilities. How ironic that surviving a summer with Madam would be so beneficial.

My first few interviews were in vain. I was either too young or didn't have enough experience – and I wasn't the *English Butler* my potential employers had in mind. But the *coup-de-grâce* always was – *no* Reference from Mrs. Young "Why not?" they asked, "What did *you* do wrong?"

But one day in late October Miss Olivia called to tell me she had found the perfect position for me in the upcoming Palm Beach Winter season. Since I had never been to Florida, the new adventure and the certainty of avoiding a winter in New York filled me with excitement and anticipation.

Miss Olivia spent an hour coaching me in her office in preparation for my interview. We went through the questions that I might be asked and what my reply should be. Miss Olivia instructed me to be sure my appearance was impeccable.

My interview with Ambassador Arthur Gardner and his wife Suzanne (née Anderson) took place in the Waldorf Towers where they were staying. Oddly enough their family name Gardner was spelled *exactly* the same way as mine.

I had visited the Waldorf Astoria Hotel with my family years earlier but had never been to the exclusive Waldorf Towers. I entered the Towers by the private entrance on East 50th Street and presented myself at the concierge's desk. When I told him my name he reasonably assumed I was family and told me to go right up.

The smiling operator took me up and pointed out the Gardner suite. I rang the doorbell and a maid opened the door and ushered me in. His Excellency, Ambassador Gardner was seated at the far end of the tastefully-decorated living room.

It appeared to me that the Ambassador was not in the best of health. Seated nearby was his attractive, visibly younger wife. Mrs. Gardner rose and invited me to sit opposite her. I gave her the letter of introduction from the agency outlining my sterling characteristics and qualifications. Since my Reference from Mrs. Young was non-existent and that fact had sabotaged my attempts to find work, Miss Olivia had already explained my situation to Mrs. Gardner.

We spoke for over twenty minutes. Mrs. Gardner summarized the requirements of the position and explained that she and her husband entertained frequently while in Palm Beach – mounting several formal dinner parties each week. She informed me that I would be working with Mr. Brian, her English Butler. She added that the duke and duchess of Windsor would be their guests for the second half of the Winter season after having spent the first half with Mrs. Young at Montsorrel. It appeared that Mrs. Gardner too had chosen to play the role of 'lady-in-waiting' to the couple.

I asked her if she knew Mrs. Young. She simply said, "Very well," and added that she and Miss Olivia had discussed the absence of her Reference.

I must have made a face or something because she laughed and said,

"The fact that you survived even half a season with Mrs. Young was recommendation enough for me."

In short, I got the job. I was hired as the Junior Butler with a salary more than double my wages at Fairholme.

When the interview ended Mrs. Gardner handed me an envelope. Inside was a plane ticket to West Palm Beach. Not bad.

Victor, the Gardners' caretaker/chauffeur met me at the airport. Dressed in my New York winter attire, I was overwhelmed by heat and humidity when we left West Palm Beach. Thank goodness for cars with air-conditioning.

When we crossed the Intracoastal Canal (known locally as Lake Worth) on the Royal Palm Bridge, I realized instantly that Palm Beach was nothing like Newport, the three-hundred-year-old New England fishing town where my so-called 'career' began.

Palm Beach was initially developed in the early twentieth century as a winter resort for the very rich. It is filled with countless luxurious homes and villas, grand hotels and Worth Avenue – an elegant promenade of fine shops and restaurants.

The Gardners' home was in the Spanish hacienda style typical of many South Florida mansions. It was a two-storied "U" shaped structure built around a central courtyard densely planted with flowers, exotic foliage and palms. A large antique Mission bell was set up in the courtyard. It was a gift to Ambassador Gardner from the Batista government when he was American Ambassador to Cuba in the 1950s.

He delighted in striking it to summon their guests to the table at formal dinner parties.

In 1910 Ambassador Arthur Gardner began his career as a businessman and financier at The Equitable Trust Company in New York. He enlisted in the U.S. Army as a private in the First World War and rose to the rank of Captain in the tank corps.

In 1925 he married Suzanne M. Anderson the daughter of John Wendell Anderson, a Detroit lawyer who was one of the twelve original stockholders in the Ford Motor Company. Anderson sold his fifty shares back to Henry Ford and his son Edsel in 1919 for twelve and a half million dollars!

During his military service he befriended Major Dwight D. Eisenhower and maintained a close relationship with the future president for many years. Upon returning to the private sector in 1926 he became a partner in the Detroit legal firm of Anderson & Gardner.

During the Second World War he was a consultant to the War Production Board and later, during the Truman administration, he was appointed special assistant to the Secretary of the Treasury, John W. Snyder.

In 1953, during Eisenhower's first presidential term, he was appointed to the post of U.S. Ambassador to Cuba in the early years of Fidel Castro's campaign to overthrow the Batista regime.

Gardner however, was strongly pro-Batista. The administration grew to view his position as an impediment to future Cuban-American relations and forced him to resign in 1957.

The Ambassador and Suzy had two daughters and a son. The couple maintained homes in Washington, D.C., Watch Hill, Rhode Island and Palm Beach.

The Gardners were not scheduled to arrive until the following week but with my arrival the full staff had gathered. It was a large staff for the relatively small house – equal in number to that of Fairholme.

It included Victor, the chauffeur/caretaker, the Head Cook and her kitchen aid, the Ambassador's valet, Mrs. Gardner's personal lady's maid and Margaret, the parlor maid/waitress who was more like a Housekeeper than a maid. She had been with the family for many years and effectively ran the house.

Last was Mr. Brian – the English Butler. He was effete to the extreme and was possessed of a most unrealistic assessment of his beauty and importance.

The house had been closed since the end of the last Winter season. During the summer, with Palm Beach virtually abandoned, Victor and his wife checked in on it frequently.

That notwithstanding, there was a great deal of work to be accomplished before the Gardners' arrival. To prepare the house itself for a 'white glove' inspection – a top to bottom deep cleaning headed the list.

Victor had maintained the grounds and courtyard throughout the summer. (A must in a climate with a twelve-month growing season.) But the pool remained to be cleaned and filled.

The Gardners' pool was on the beach and was accessed by a tunnel under South Ocean Boulevard. At the time there were only two such tunnels in Palm Beach. The second was at Mrs. Post's Mar-a-Lago and led to the Bath and Tennis Club.

Provisioning the larder with all the basic food items and wines and spirits came next. The point of all the fuss was that when the Gardners arrived they would feel as if they had never been away.

When they appeared after Thanksgiving, the house was completely in order and humming with life.

The reason for hiring me was that Mrs. Gardner preferred to have two men capable of performing the luncheon and formal dinner services – Mr. Brian, the Butler and me, the Junior Butler. It was an unusual arrangement since the pairing of the Butler with a parlor-maid/waitress was customary.

Mr. Brian was an obnoxious man. Like Valdemar, he was a snob but didn't allude to noble forebears. Rather, he continually bragged about previously having worked for this or that 'Royal' in England.

He was pudgy, in his mid-to-late fifties, with a very affected way of speaking. And nothing, absolutely nothing was to his liking, the silver – not old enough, the pantry – not large enough, the dinner wines – not up to his standards and the final affront was – his bedroom didn't face the ocean.

One evening, just prior to a formal dinner party, Mr. Brian and Mrs. Gardner had a loud disagreement in the Butler's pantry as to just how a certain cocktail should be prepared. Unable to convince Mrs. Gardner of *his* obviously superior technique in this matter, Mr. Brian turned and left the room. That was the beginning of the end of Mr. Brian.

On his day off one weekday morning, Mr. Brian decided to have a stroll on the public beach to get a *bit* of color. An hour or so after he left the phone rang in the pantry. Margaret answered.

It was an officer of the Palm Beach Police Department. He said that Mr. Brian was in their custody. He was charged with indecent exposure and had been arrested while strolling down the beach wearing what could only be described as a *codpiece.*

Margaret, who loathed him as much as I did, transferred the call to Ambassador Gardner and then began laughing hysterically. Then, with lip-smacking relish, she related the delicious details of the phone call. Before you knew it, we were both rolling on the floor (so to speak) shrieking with laughter.

I bonded instantly with Margaret since she was free of the usual hang-ups held by the 'old-school' domestics like those at Fairholme – especially Flora. I frequently found myself in side-splitting conversations with her in the staff dining room regarding Mrs. Young and my Newport experience.

Victor drove the Ambassador to the Police Station in order to bail Mr. Brian out. Later, during our staff lunch hour the police delivered Mr. Brian wrapped in a large white beach towel. He hurried up to his room and was not seen again until the next morning.

Then the officer handed Margaret a package and left. Everyone's curiosity was aroused. What could this mysterious package contain? Margaret opened it gingerly and – lo and behold, it was – *the codpiece!*

It was a triangular bit of cloth on a wire frame attached to a curving metal rod with a button hook of sorts at its end which I guess, passed between Mr. Brian's legs and anchored at the base of his spine. It had no back panel so his rather flabby behind was completely exposed – hence his arrest. The apparatus reminded me of a fig leaf on a classic statue.

The next morning Mr. Brian arrived at staff breakfast in his full Butler's livery and acted as if nothing had happened – very 'stiff-upper-lip' and all that.

One morning Margaret took me aside and told me that I had to give up my bedroom and move to a boarding house a mile away on Royal Palm Way. The reason behind this unexpected and unwelcome news was that the duke and duchess were having problems at Montsorrel.

The couple, clotheshorses that they were, never traveled without their own personal maid and valet. Their many steamer trunks afforded them countless changes of attire for each day's social schedule. That was the problem.

They originally planned to spend the first half of the Winter season at Mrs. Young's and the second half at the Gardner's, so it was logical to expect that the trunks of clothes be delivered to Montsorrel first.

However, during the delivery several of the walls leading to the newly-completed 'Royal Suite' were damaged. Perfectionist Mrs. Young was furious and ordered their trunks instantly removed. This triggered a frantic call to the Gardners.

It was decided that after the trunks were unpacked they would be sent to the Gardners. It made perfect sense since the Windsors were scheduled to stay with the Gardners for the second half of the season.

Unbeknownst to me, I had been scheduled to lose my bedroom at the Gardners with the arrival of the Windsors. Two of the four guest bedroom suites would accommodate the Windsors and the other two would house their lady's maid and valet. My bedroom, now shortly to become the trunk's storage room would have, upon the Windsors arrival, become the 'pressing room' for the lady's maid and the valet. So one way or another I would shortly be homeless.

The situation was not promising. I could have demanded to be housed on the property as that was the original agreement at my initial interview. However, the result of that action could result in my being discharged – again. I reassessed my options and decided to make the best of it and I moved to the boarding house on Royal Palm Way.

The difficulty with this unexpected situation was that in the course of my long workday, I had nowhere to take a break and relax for even half an hour. My day began at seven-thirty in the morning and lasted well into the evening. When there were large dinner parties, I worked until the early morning hours of the next day. One day I worked nineteen hours without a break.

Another problem with my off-premises sleeping setup was that Victor had to pick me up every morning and take me back to the boarding house at the end of the day. At times when he couldn't, I called a taxi. And Mrs. Gardner, who was quite agreeable at my interview in New

York had turned taciturn and distant in Palm Beach. Several times when I approached her with a question, she would raise up her right hand to silence me, and say, "Ask Mr. Brian."

"Fat chance!" thought I.

One afternoon, shortly after staff lunch, I entered the staff dining room and noticed a young man seated at the far end of the room in one of the large reading chairs. Lowering his newspaper and gazing over it, he said to me,

"So you're the *new boy* in town!"

It was Gordon Jones, the Ambassador's former valet and now the valet and first Under-Butler at Mrs. Post's estate, Mar-a-Lago. He was Welsh and in his early thirties. He was blonde, five-foot-eight with an athletic, swimmer's body.

During our initial conversation Gordon told me he had his own car, a Mustang and asked if I would like to take a drive around Palm Beach on my day off to view the sights. Who could turn down such an offer? I never had anything special to do on my day off and so his suggestion was both intriguing and most welcome.

Two days later Gordon and his Mustang arrived after breakfast for our adventure. We drove through all Palm Beach and he showed me a multitude of mansions including Mrs. Young's new palace, Montsorrel.

To finish my tour we drove by Mar-a-Lago at 1100 South Ocean Boulevard. I was beyond impressed. Then he invited me to lunch at the Breakers, a magnificent, Italian-palazzo-style hotel on South County Road. I mentioned that I was wary of running into Mrs. Young or Mrs. Gardner there. Gordon laughed and said,

"Relax Tom. You won't see them there. The only time they venture out at mid-day would be to lunch with friends at a 'Members Only' club like the Everglades or the Bath and Tennis. They never go anywhere open to the public."

"Anyway," he continued, "I heard about your Mr. Brian. That was something else – to say nothing of his confronting Mrs. Gardner over to how to mix a drink."

"Do you know everything that goes on in Palm Beach?" I asked.

"Of course," he replied.

We did laugh over Mr. Brian's ridiculous dilemma. It seemed everyone in the domestic line in Palm Beach was gossiping about him. Gordon and I had instant rapport. Like myself, he was objective about working for the rich. We both believed that they were like everyone else – only with a lot more money.

After lunch Gordon continued the tour of Palm Beach. In the late afternoon we went to his apartment on the top floor of Mar-a-Lago's 'guest cottage.' There, over a scotch and soda or two, he related story after story about the delights of Marjorie Merriweather Post's Palm Beach home.

When evening arrived we decided to have a light snack in West Palm Beach and then hit one or two of the local 'watering-holes' that Gordon thought I might enjoy. It was a wonderful day.

Two days later Gordon appeared once again in the staff dining room and asked to speak to me alone. He was direct and to the point. He told me that the position of fourth footman (Under-Butler) would shortly become available at Mar-a-Lago and if I wanted it he would put in a good word with Mr. Moffat, Mrs. Post's Steward – who was in charge of hiring and discharging staff. Gordon was first Under-Butler and was in fact the third most-powerful member of the male staff. Only Mr. Moffat, the Steward and Mr. Livingston, the Butler were superior to him.

Gordon said that my hiring was a sure thing. He reiterated that working for Mrs. Post was an amazing experience and an opportunity not to be missed.

I immediately said "YES!"

Once again, I was to appear before a potential employer without References. Lucky for me Mrs. Post did not concern herself with the hiring or discharging of staff. That was Mr. Moffat's bailiwick. When I entered his office for my interview on the morning of my day off, he looked up, smiled and said, "Welcome to Mar-a-Lago Thomas."

Later that day I went back to the Gardners and told Margaret that I had found a new position and would be leaving shortly. She was aware that I was unhappy with the sleeping arrangements and also knew that I loathed working with the preposterous Mr. Brian. She asked me to wait a bit since the Gardners were already interviewing a new Butler and Mr. Brian would soon be history. I said I could stay one week more as I had already accepted my new position at Mar-a-Lago.

Considering the exhaustive training I received under the direction of Mrs. Young, I knew, with Margaret's help, I could have taken over Mr. Brian's position and done a superb job. But realistically, I knew the duke and duchess were going to move from Montsorrel to the Gardners in less than three weeks and Mrs. Gardner, for some silly reason, absolutely had to have a born-and-bred, real *English Butler* for them.

In any case, I found the lure of being part of Mar-a-Lago impossible to resist and realized that yet another chapter of my unusual field of employment awaited.

Chapter Four

Marjorie Merriweather Post

Shall we dance?

My move to Mar-a-Lago was easily accomplished since I never fully unpacked my two suitcases. So with the help of Gordon and his Mustang – I said good riddance to the boarding house on Royal Palm Way and was off to Mar-a-Lago.

In 1924 Marjorie Merriweather Post and her second husband Edward Francis (E.F.) Hutton discovered the ideal site for their second Palm Beach mansion – a seventeen-acre tract of vacant land stretching from the Atlantic Ocean on the east to Lake Worth on the west.

The estate would be called Mar-a-Lago (Sea-to-Lake) for the obvious reason. They hired Marion Sims Wyeth, one of Palm Beach's foremost architects, to design the main house. Wyeth, a graduate of Princeton and the École des Beaux Arts had designed 'Hogarcito,' the Huttons' first Palm Beach house.

Working together, Wyeth and Mrs. Hutton determined the size, location and floor plan of the new mansion. But Mrs. Hutton was not taken with the typical Beaux Arts structure Wyeth had in mind nor did she want a Mediterranean-style villa in the manner of Addison Mizner – variations of which were cropping up all over Palm Beach at that time.

The problem was solved when Florenz Ziegfeld and his wife Billie Burke, close friends of the Huttons introduced them to the extravagant 'Ziegfeld Follies' set designer and architect, Joseph Urban.

Urban's impressive portfolio included projects for Austria's Emperor, Franz Josef and Egypt's last Ottoman viceroy, Khedive Abbas Hilmi II. In New York he designed astonishing sets for the Metropolitan Opera and of course, for Ziegfeld's famed 'Follies.'

Urban designed a crescent-shaped, one-hundred-and-fifteen-room structure fronting Lake Worth having a seventy-five-foot tower in a hybrid Hispano-Moresque/Austrian Secession style. The gardens would be lushly planted and a nine-hole golf course was included. Mrs. Hutton was delighted with Urban's over-the-top design and construction soon began. Money was no object.

Thirty-six thousand antique Spanish tiles, some dating to the fifteenth century were used as wall decoration. Antique terra-cotta roof tiles were purchased in Cuba. Rare marbles came from Italy.

Gifted designer though he was, Urban was not really an architect so Mrs. Hutton asked Wyeth to come back and design the more mundane aspects such as plumbing, electricity and other necessities.

On arrival my I was assigned a room in Men's Hall. It was spotlessly clean and, unlike my room at Mrs. Young's or at the Gardner's where all the staff rooms were furnished with a hodge-podge of second-hand furniture, it had a matching suite of good quality furniture and a medicine cabinet and a sink. The communal showers and toilet facilities were modern and impeccable with the atmosphere of a country-club.

Gordon told me not to concern myself with cleaning my room. He explained that Mrs. Post felt it was most practical to have a dedicated team of two maids and one houseman attend to the staff bedrooms daily.

This remarkable concept of 'staff for the staff' is rooted in an English system used in formal houses where a *pecking order* of upper and lower staff and their respective duties existed.

Mar-a-Lago mandated a large live-in staff. All the single men lived in Men's Hall except for the three chauffeurs who lived above the garage. The unmarried female staff (who out-numbered their male counterparts) lived in Woman's Hall. Married couples had slightly larger quarters.

Mr. Moffat, the Steward and his wife, Mr. Livingston, the Head Butler and his wife (the Head Cook) had suites on the Lake Worth side of the property. My new friend Gordon, the First Under-Butler, had a comfortable suite on the upper floor of the so-called 'Guest Cottage.'

When I arrived Mar-a-Lago had forty-five live-in staff – *two* cooks, *eight* kitchen aids, *three* chauffeurs, *four* footmen and numerous parlor-maids and upstairs and downstairs maids.

Everyone worked seven mornings a week. But it was not as awful as it sounds since every other day after lunch, half of the in-house staff took the afternoon off. However, on Thursdays when Mrs. Post staged her weekly 'Square and Round' dinner-dance, the entire household staff worked the whole day. True to her Midwestern roots, the worldly Mrs. Post enjoyed the simple, down-to-earth pleasure of American square dancing.

At both Mar-a-Lago and Hillwood, her home in Washington, the staff had a chauffeured station-wagon at their disposal on their half-day off. After staff lunch, our Australian chauffeur Alfred, drove us across the bridge to West Palm Beach to shop or go to the movies and return to bring us back in the early evening. No taxis needed. Since the mostly female older staff preferred to remain at home, the staff station-wagon was rarely crowded. In addition, Mrs. Post reserved a part of her private, ocean-front beach specifically for the staff. So when I had no reason to go to town, I perfected my suntan. Gordon was right, working for Mrs. Post was *absolutely amazing*.

Privately, the entire staff referred to Mrs. Post as 'Mother.' It was a richly-deserved term of affection because of the outstanding working conditions she provided.

Mr. Livingston supervised all four Under-Butlers and three housemen. The Under-Butlers were responsible for serving the breakfasts, lunches and dinners. When, for a large dinner party, additional staff was required, Alfred, the chauffeur functioned as a fifth Under-Butler.

The four Under-Butlers had other duties as well – Gordon was the valet and cared for the male Guests' clothing. Arthur (a most gentle soul who loved the comic strip 'Peanuts') passed his days polishing a most impressive selection of sterling and vermeil flatware and hollowware. A good deal of it had been taken from Mrs. Post's ocean-going yacht, the 'Sea Cloud' before she sold it to the dictator-president of The Dominican Republic, Raphael Trujillo. Alex maintained the dining room and the entrance hall.

My job as fourth Under-Butler was to keep the Butlers' pantry organized and well-stocked. The Guest's preferences with regard to the time and content of their breakfast had been written and delivered to the Butler's pantry the evening before and Mrs. Livingston's kitchen complied with all their preferences. This one wanted his eggs scrambled – that one hard-boiled – another one requested extra crisp bacon – another wanted whole wheat toast – and so on – *ad infinitum*.

Since the breakfast trays were assembled in the Butler's pantry before being taken up to the guest rooms a high degree of coordination between the kitchen and pantry was required. It often drove me nuts!

Mrs. Post's Social Secretary was Mrs. Margaret Voigt who, like Miss Coffin at Fairholme, was very impressed with her position. She supplied the staff with a daily memorandum noting Mother's routine for the day. Everyone, including Mother's family members, disliked her and avoided her whenever possible.

The Post fortune had remarkable origins. In 1891 Marjorie's father Charles William (C.W.) Post checked into the Western Health Reform Institute (later the Battle Creek Sanitarium) in Battle Creek, Michigan. He was a hyperactive thirty-seven-year old native of Springfield, Illinois and was suffering from a breakdown brought about by his unsuccessful struggles as a traveling salesman, inventor and entrepreneur.

Escorted by his wife, Ella Merriweather Post and their four-year old daughter Marjorie, C.W. entered Dr. John Harvey Kellogg's Institute – the best-known health establishment in the country. The Institute provided dietary therapy – sugar, meat and caffeine were banned – whole grain concoctions were the medicine. C.W.'s financial situation however, obliged the family to move into an inexpensive boarding house nearby.

Nine months of dietary therapy did not cure C.W.'s ills. However, he met Mary Baker Eddy, the founder of Christian Science, in Battle Creek. She preached that healing comes from neither medicine nor diet – but from the mind of God. Under her influence, his symptoms miraculously eased.

With the small amount of money Ella inherited, C.W. decided to open his own sanatorium called 'La Vita Inn' in Battle Creek. There, therapy was based on a mixture of diet, Christian-Science principles and hypnotism. It was moderately successful.

In 1895 C.W. created 'Postum,' a caffeine-free coffee substitute made of pulverized roasted grains and molasses. He advertised it prodigiously and stressed the health benefits of his Postum over the toxicity of coffee. The product soon caught the public's fancy and orders poured in. By 1902, the year C.W. and Ella separated, C.W. had become a multi-millionaire.

In 1905 eighteen-year-old Marjorie married the scion of one of Greenwich, Connecticut's founding families, Edward Bennett Close. He was a Columbia Law School graduate, a lawyer and a stockbroker. C.W. had by this time constructed a home for Marjorie and her future family in Greenwich, Connecticut named 'The Boulders,'

The newlyweds moved in and eventually Adelaide and Eleanor, Mrs. Post's daughters with Close, were born there.

C.W.'s health continued to deteriorate and he committed suicide in his California home in May 1914. After months of legal bickering with Leila, C.W.'s second wife, the document leaving the entire Postum Cereal Company to twenty-seven-year-old Marjorie was located. Although it was exceptional for the period, C.W. had educated his daughter in the company's management.

Marjorie was bored with her role as a Greenwich homemaker (albeit with a large staff) and decided to commute from Greenwich to New York City where she took over the management of the Postum Cereal Company.

Commuting was burdensome and so the Closes rented I. Townsend Burden's impressive, five-story Beaux Arts mansion on Fifth Avenue and East 92nd Street for a year. They bought it in 1916. During the First World War Marjorie began furnishing the house with fine antiques while Edward was in the Army in Europe.

She befriended art dealers and experts in New York and grew increasingly knowledgeable. In 1919 the Closes divorced and a year later Marjorie married Edward Francis (E.F.) Hutton, a Wall Street broker and financier. Another daughter, Nedinia (Dina) Marjorie Hutton was born in 1923.

That year E.F. Hutton was named chairman of the board of the Postum Cereal Company and in 1925 the company headquarters moved from Battle Creek to New York City. The company began to diversify into other food products and changed its name to The Postum Company in 1927.

The name was changed once again with the purchase of Clarence Birdseye's frozen food company to The General Foods Corporation. General Foods became one of the world's largest and most important food conglomerates. Mr. Hutton served as chairman of the board of General Foods until 1935 when he and Marjorie were divorced. In 1936 Marjorie became one of the first women to sit on the board of a major American corporation.

Mother employed hundreds of people. In addition to the forty-five who traveled with her to and from her three residences, there were year-round maintenance men, gardeners and an army of security guards for all three properties. She also retained a crew of four for the Merriweather, her Vickers Viscount turbo-jet. Before selling her huge, four-mast, ocean-going yacht, the Sea Cloud, she maintained a crew of seventy-three men.

No one except Mr. Moffat, the Livingstons and Mrs. Voigt were permitted to initiate a conversation with Mother. If she asked a question of any of the other staff member it was to be answered – "Yes, Mrs. Post" or "No, Mrs. Post." She was *never* to be addressed as 'Madam.'

Mother married four times. Ergo, she had four different surnames. If one chose to recite them all together they would read:

Mrs. Marjorie Close Hutton Davies May.

After divorcing her fourth husband Herbert May (CEO of General Motors) she decided to reclaim her maiden name – Post. But since 'Miss Post' was not appropriate for a woman of her age and position – she chose to be addressed as 'Mrs. Post.'

My first Thursday arrived. The weekly Square and Round dinner-dance for approximately one hundred and fifty guests was scheduled for that evening. Preparations for the elaborate, well-orchestrated ritual monopolized the staff for the entire day. My work day began at six forty-five.

By seven-fifteen I was bathed, groomed, dressed and having my breakfast in the most impressive Butler's pantry in all Palm Beach.

The resident guests' breakfast trays had been prepared the night before and were sent up to the rooms of the single women and married couples by nine-thirty.

Married male guests could breakfast in their rooms with their wives or in the Monkey Room. Many chose the Monkey Room. It was a delightful place to start the day and get to know to other male guests since single male guests were *obliged* to breakfast there. The Monkey room held up to eight people and was also used for private family luncheons.

The Monkey Room derived its name from the numerous carvings of monkeys that swarmed over its walls. The carvings, made of Oölite (a local coral stone) were designed and executed by the Viennese sculptor Franz Barwig and his son Franz the Younger, who worked on site at Mar-a-Lago for almost three years sculpting parrots, monkeys and other subjects.

Guest breakfast over, the full-throttle, fifteen-hour weekly Square and Round dinner-dance-day, began. And what a day it was!

The Steward, Mr. Moffat, the Butler, Mr. Livingston, the four Under-Butlers, two chauffeurs, three housemen, sweet little Alma (who was in charge of the table linens) and a multitude of the upstairs, downstairs and parlor-maids joined in the chore of setting the Square and Round circus in motion.

The kitchen staff consisted of Mrs. Livingston, the Head-Cook, her under-cook and all eight kitchen aids. The entire staff knew their duties regarding this weekly event that took place in all Mother's homes since the 1950s.

After staff lunch ended, the task force consisting of Mr. and Mrs. Livingston and Mr. Moffat entered high gear. But it was only with the arrival of the supplemental serving staff that I realized the astonishing amount of labor this weekly undertaking mandated.

From one hundred to one hundred fifty guests were expected and so ten additional waiters would be required plus more personnel for the Butler's pantry and kitchen. Many of the day-help who worked outside in the gardens assisted in setting-up a multitude of tables and chairs in both the dining room and outside on the crescent-shaped covered loggia. At the same time, the china, silver, stemware and linens needed were expeditiously assembled and then, placed.

The skill and ease with which this event was assembled would be the envy of any five-star hotel, not to mention the other private homes in Palm Beach. To see a house, albeit a grand one, being quickly and completely transformed for just one evening's event astounded me.

In the dining room, eight round tables, four on each side, flanked the world-famous, fully-extended, four-thousand-pound, inlaid marble 'Medici' extension table. Mrs. Post ordered the custom-built table for Mar-a-Lago in 1927 from the Medici Marble Works of Florence, Italy.

It has a pietra-dura top of eleven different varieties of marble (some in the shape of fruit spilling from shell-like cornucopia on its borders,) and six removable 'leaves' which, when in place, extended the table to a length of twenty-nine feet. (It is now at Hillwood in Washington.)

An additional eight tables were placed outside on the covered loggia. Mother and her Guest of Honor were joined by one fortunate couple and seated at a table at the southernmost end of the living room opposite the Venetian fireplace.

Dinner was served buffet style. Mrs. Livingston and her team of kitchen aids had toiled for several days preparing the splendid feast. Gracing the entire length of the table, the display of the food was right out of a Versailles feast with massive floral arrangements and candelabra. Fifty years later I still recall the astounding effect that experience had on me.

Whether it was a 'small' dinner party for eighteen or a large event such as the Square and Round, all the Post residences had a strict, never-to-be-broken rule, they all ended *promptly* at eleven when Mother retired to her quarters.

Guests were instructed to arrive between seven and seven-twenty. Many had their private chauffeurs but for those who didn't, carhops parked their vehicles in the lower parking area by Lake Worth.

Mother made her grand entrance at exactly seven-thirty, greeted her guests and the party began with a cocktail hour in the grand living room.

Those that couldn't fit into the huge room made their way to the outside loggia and the gardens. Since Mother disapproved of drunkenness, alcohol consumption was monitored. It was expected that guests would limit themselves to two cocktails before dinner. However, aware that hard liquor would not be flowing freely at the Square and Round, several guests imbibed before the party started – or secretly brought their own flasks.

Occasionally, there was shortage of either men or women dance partners. To solve this problem Mrs. Voigt was responsible for hiring the necessary number of accomplished extra dancers to attend. Seriously vetted by the Palm Beach agency, they were required to arrive at seven and stay until eleven when the Square and Round ended with Mother's departure. They were obliged to participate in the cocktail hour, the dinner and of course – the dancing.

The extra men were often over-forty, retired actors who used this as their Winter season 'vocation.' The women, usually younger were on the hunt for wealthy widowers. Needless to say they all coveted this desirable, paid stint where good food and opportunity abounded.

By and large they all behaved well since – had anyone, a hired dancer (or even a male or female guest) crossed Mother's *propriety* line they would be permanently banned from future Mar-a-Lago events. I remember at one Square and Round Mr. Livingston asked me to *politely* direct a male guest (who had obviously had one too many) to quiet down and remember where he was. He obeyed, but was probably never invited back to Mar-a-Lago.

The entire staff knew that this bunch could always spot a tray of caviar as soon as it left the pantry. Therefore, all the caviar servers were specifically instructed by Mr. Livingston to avoid them whenever possible.

One Thursday evening I was partnered with Alex, the third Under-Butler. Alex was Danish and somewhere in his late thirties. He would occasionally have a nip or two before an evening's work to 'relax' him. When the cocktail part of the dinner-dance was well underway, Alex and I were walking back to the pantry to replenish our trays (mine was a caviar tray). It was then that Alex requested that we switch trays. You see, passing the caviar always made one the center of attention, which Alex obviously enjoyed. It was okay with me. However, my new 'mixed' tray took a few moments longer to arrange. That being the case, Alex was several feet ahead of me on his way out through the pantry's doors (one OUT – one IN) that led to the formal dining room.

As Alex exited the pantry with his caviar tray his judgment was slightly *off*. I can't count how many times he had gone through those doors – weighed down by the heavy sterling silver, food-laden platters which Mother had retrieved from the Sea Cloud before she sold it to Raphael Trujillo. Alex attempted to leave through IN door and so when his tray struck the immobile door it became instantly airborne. He somehow managed to catch it in midair but unfortunately all the caviar hit the floor. What a mess! Lucky for Alex, Mr. Livingston neither saw nor learned of the event.

Mother and her dinner guests were first on line at the buffet. When dinner had ended, everyone walked to the Dance Pavilion. Mother hired musicians and local square dance callers. Ramrod straight and elegant in a peasant blouse and a long, flowing skirt Mother danced almost every dance. Everyone was expected to join her in both square and ballroom (round) dances.

At ten-thirty, the foundation of the Post fortune 'Postum,' C.W. Post's caffeine-free coffee substitute was served in the Dance Pavilion. Tea was available for those who wished to avoid the salubrious, but evil-tasting, brew.

The beverages were accompanied by vast quantities of finger sandwiches. Earlier in the day Mr. Livingston and two footmen (I was usually one of them) had prepared these tiny, yet elegant sandwiches with assembly-line precision in the Butler's pantry. We made dozens and dozens of them, never really believing that they would all be eaten – and they weren't.

By half past eleven, the tables had been put away, all the dishes and glasses washed and stowed and the pantry set-up for the next day's breakfast service. The extra staff had been paid and departed. All that was left was the clearing of any leftover food from the Dance Pavilion. I always volunteered to help.

My interest for taking part in that final task was the chance to get hold of the uneaten finger sandwiches. I had Mr. Livingston's permission to rescue the little delicacies as they would soon be tossed in the trash. Such a pity! So I carefully wrapped each few in a foil packet, dashed back to my room, jumped into my ever-so-snug jeans, my penny-loafers (no socks) and my slightly-worn Izod shirt, and made my way to a waiting taxi that whisked me to my adoring fans at 'The Turf,' a popular watering hole in West Palm Beach.

'The Turf' was an oasis where the counterculture of the 1960s was alive and flourishing and the changing social mores of the time were evident. I met and socialized not only with the young staff members of the grand estates but also with the scions of Palm Beach Society themselves. A noteworthy aspect of those chance meetings was that they were often with the same people I had served just a few hours earlier.

So, my Thursday evening arrival with the finger sandwiches was a well-known and eagerly-anticipated *happening*. I became 'the Guest of Honor' and my drinks were all comped.

In addition to twelve Square and Round events that winter, Mother hosted three Saturday-evening, formal dinner parties for the *crème de la crème* of Palm Beach society and their notable houseguests. Those dinners were the highlights of the 1967 Winter season and were held in Mar-a-Lago's formal dining room which was inspired by a room in the Chigi palace in Rome.

Everything about these formal dinners attested to Mother's high standard of excellence. The marble dining table was extended to its maximum length to accommodate twenty-eight people. It was embellished with one of her numerous services of Sèvres porcelain, her 'Queen Margherita' Venetian stemware that consisted of four distinct goblet sizes for each setting, her vermeil place plates, flatware and two massive six-branch candelabra. A magnificent floral arrangement graced its center. A calligraphed menu and place card in vermeil holders provided the finishing touch.

Yardsticks were used to ensure that everything on the table was equidistant from the center and that each place setting was precisely sixteen inches from its neighbor. Mr. Livingston, the four Under-Butlers and Alfred (the staff chauffeur who doubled as a fifth Under-Butler when necessary) manned all three dinner parties.

Mr. Livingston who valued my appearance and bearing frequently assigned high-profile guests to me at these dinners. Two stand out.

At the first, after the alcohol-deprived cocktail hour ended and the guests were seated at their designated places, Mr. Livingston assigned me to cover the most important guest of that evening – Mrs. Rose Kennedy.

That night Mrs. Kennedy was wearing, in the fashion of the day, a gown with an elaborately beaded bodice. She had been seated between two male dinner partners, one of whom was known to gesticulate wildly with his arms when making a point.

The first course was the usual cold consommé. As I approached Mrs. Kennedy I stood back to allow her neighbor's overly demonstrative movements to cease. When they did I snatched the opportunity to place the consommé on Mrs. Kennedy's place plate. To my horror he gesticulated wildly once again and hit my arm. There was nothing I could do to prevent what was to come.

Holding onto the bowl's under-plate with one hand, I attempted to capture the liquid that had leapt out of it with my other hand. Nonetheless, the consommé splashed into the air and then into Mrs. Kennedy's beaded bodice.

At first, she seemed surprised and then, as if this happened on a regular basis, she began to dab her chest with a napkin. In a semi panic I set the half-empty soup bowl in front of her and ran immediately to Mr. Livingston.

I explained my horrendous situation to him. He immediately took charge and did what I eventually began to think of as a 'Livingston.' He reached for a fresh napkin, placed it on a small tray, and instructed me to go back to Mrs. Kennedy, offer her the fresh napkin, and say nothing.

I of course, followed his instructions. After accepting the fresh napkin Mrs. Kennedy smiled up at me and then continued to dab herself with it and – lo and behold it was all over. What had seemed to me an unbelievable disaster turned out to be another moment to be cherished.

My second formal dinner transpired a month later. The duke and duchess of Windsor were the evening's notable guests. My former employer, the soon-to-be-widowed Suzy Gardner, their hostess at that time was there as well. Mrs. Young was not.

Mr. Livingston stationed me to the area that included the duke of Windsor. I found it quite interesting that at Mar-a-Lago, unlike at Fairholme and I assume at Montsorrel as well, the duke and duchess were *not* treated as Royalty and seated at both heads of the table. They were seated diagonally opposite each other mid-table. Here, Mother sat at the head of the table. It was after all – *her* table.

The duke had the habit of taking off his slippers when participating in a long, formal dinner party. But this time without realizing it, the woman seated next to him kicked one of them out of his reach accidentally.

At dinner's mid-point the duke waved me over and whispered that his slipper had 'somehow gotten away from him' and would I 'be good enough to retrieve it?' I answered, 'Of course, Sir' and I made a beeline directly to Mr. Livingston who was standing behind Mother supervising the entire event. As I walked quickly towards him, I noticed the duchess staring at the duke and then at me, a look of high anxiety on her face. I had heard she watched him like a hawk, especially at social functions.

Always in control, Mr. Livingston instructed me to, 'Place a spoon on small tray then go to the duke's seat and accidentally drop the spoon on the floor next to him. When you bend down to retrieve it, locate the slipper and put it next to his foot and then touch his foot with it.' I did that – problem solved. I nodded to the duchess, she smiled at me. Just another classic 'Livingston.'

One day I was assigned a small luncheon in the Monkey Room. The attendees were Mother, her youngest daughter Dina Merrill, Cliff Robertson, Dina's husband at the time and the severe and generally disliked Mrs. Voigt, Mother's Social Secretary.

Nearing eighty, Mother was plagued with a severe loss of hearing. For small, private affairs like this one a remarkable sound system was designed to permit her to hear and therefore engage in the conversation. Her guests spoke into a microphone and an amplifier/speaker facing her on the table, allowed her to hear them. She also had a pair of custom-designed hearing aids cleverly disguised as earrings.

The three luncheon guests were seated and were waiting for Mother's arrival. Mr. Livingston and I stood at the ready. She entered with her usual flourish and sat at the head of the table. Once seated, she realized something was amiss and frowned slightly. The always-observant Livingston was at her side in a flash.

She whispered something to him and a moment later he signaled me to his side. He told me that Mother had forgotten the earrings and her luncheon rings. He instructed me to make my way to her private quarters as quickly as possible and obtain the items from Eva, her personal maid. It was a first for me. You see, unless one had a specific task to perform in that part of the house, the private quarters at Mar-a-Lago were strictly off-limits to everyone.

Mr. Livingston phoned Eva and she met me at the door to Mother's quarters and handed me the forgotten items. When I returned Mr. Livingston handed me a small silver tray with a folded napkin on it. He told me to put the earrings and rings on the napkin and present them to Mother. The hearing-aid earrings were solid gold and the rings would have made Harry Winston blanch.

Mother planned to celebrate her eightieth birthday on March 15th. Celebrations were being organized in Washington D.C. For the week of festivities, Mother planned to fly to Washington on her plane, the Merriweather and take up residence at Hillwood, her home there.

With Mr. Livingston's help, Mother selected nine members of the staff to accompany her on the Merriweather and at Hillwood. These included Mrs. Voigt and her assistant Laura, Mother's personal maid Eva, Mr. and Mrs. Livingston and all four Under-Butlers including Gordon and me! We were all needed to supplement Hillwood's skeletal Winter staff.

When the travel day arrived a veritable cortege of cars, two with Mother and her personal staff, others with the necessary staff uniforms and personal items and others carrying the trunks with Mother's gowns and furs, stopped on the tarmac in front of the ramp to the Merriweather.

The Merriweather, designed to accommodate forty-four, had been transformed into a long living room, replete with tables, club chairs and a large sofa where Mother sat. There also was a full galley offering refreshments. When we landed at the Washington airport, we were met by an equally large number of vehicles which whisked to Hillwood us by way of Rock Creek Parkway.

My first glimpse of the stately Georgian-style mansion is forever imprinted on my memory. Surrounded by formal and informal gardens replete with fountains and statuary it was named for Mother's mansion in Brookville, Long Island that she had shared with her second husband, E.F. Hutton. In 1951 the original Hillwood mansion was absorbed into Long Island University's C.W. Post campus and was eventually torn down.

The staff quarters at Hillwood were in a separate building near the mansion. When I was finished unpacking Gordon came by and took me into the mansion. He introduced me to Gus Modig (known as Mr. Gus,) the Head Butler, I later learned that he never traveled to Mother's other homes, but always stayed at Hillwood.

Excluding me, all the staff had worked at Hillwood before and easily slipped back into their accustomed duties and routines. Gordon was the house valet, Arthur was in charge of the silver, which was kept in a large, walk-in combination safe off the Butler's pantry and Alex took care of the dining room and entrance hall.

I was in charge of a slightly smaller Butler's pantry. The adjoining linen room housed a vast hoard of lace tablecloths, napkins, etc. As at Mar-a-Lago each set was wrapped, tied with a red satin ribbon and indexed in a large scrapbook with photographs and typed descriptions of each. Mother's organizational skills were once again quite evident.

With Mr. Gus's permission Gordon took me on a tour of the mansion's first floor. Mother intended Hillwood to be not only her Washington home but also a Museum that showcased her collections of eighteenth-century French art and the priceless art of Imperial Russia.

In the 1920s in order to broaden her knowledge of French decorative art, she had consulted Sir Joseph Duveen, an expert in European Old Master paintings and decorative arts and one of the world's leading art dealers. (His best known patrons were J.P. Morgan, John D, Rockefeller, Jr. and Henry Clay Frick.)

Mrs. Post purchased Hillwood in 1955 shortly after her divorce from Ambassador Davies. She remodeled and enlarged the thirty-six-room Georgian-style mansion to suit her needs. There was a grand entry hall, a French drawing room, a formal dining room, a breakfast room, two libraries and a pavilion.

In addition to these there was a hexagonal room with lit showcases exhibiting her collection of Russian porcelain. There was a separate room housing her Russian icons and eighty Fabergé pieces including two Imperial Easter Eggs. She bought the nucleus of her Russian collection in the late 1930s while living in the Soviet Union with her third husband Joseph E. Davies, the U.S. Ambassador to the Soviet Union.

She eventually willed Hillwood and all its contents to the Smithsonian Institution.

The entry hall was splendid. Mrs. Post wanted the first room one entered to evoke her collecting passions – the arts of eighteenth century France and Imperial Russia. The hall had an imposing eighteenth-century style French wrought iron and gilt-bronze staircase. On its walls hung portraits of the Russian Czars. There were two commodes by one of France's celebrated 18th-century cabinetmakers, Jean-Henri Riesener. Both were in the entry hall (including the one she had purchased from Duveen in 1931.)

New York's French and Company furnished the majestic Louis XV rock crystal chandelier. When the massive fixture needed to be cleaned it was lowered to floor level. Mother's insurance company was informed of the day and the premium was raised for that day alone.

Gordon and I entered the fifteen-foot high dining room from the Butler's pantry. It too was designed by French and Company and featured Louis XV-style carved and gilded oak paneling. The drawing room down the hall was even more extraordinary:

Above a white marble and gilt-bronze eighteenth-century French mantelpiece hung a nineteenth-century portrait of Eugénie, the last Empress of France by Franz Xaver Winterhalter. A suite of canapés and chairs created by Georges Jacob, one of the most prominent of Parisian eighteenth- and early nineteenth-century craftsmen filled the room. A second important seating group was purchased from French and Company in 1955. It had been commissioned in 1784 by Louis XVI and Marie Antoinette. It was upholstered with floral Gobelins tapestries designed by

Louis Tessier. Eighteenth-century Beauvais tapestries designed by François Boucher and bought from Duveen in the 1920s adorned the walls.

Between the south windows stood the famed Roentgen desk, often dubbed the 'Marie Antoinette' desk. Mother's daughter, Dina Merrill has told of her pleasure exploring the secret drawers of this masterpiece as a child. The chair next to it has a more decided pedigree since it is branded 'Garde Meuble de la Reine' indicating that it belonged to Marie Antoinette. Gordon said the French government wanted it back but Mother declined. In any case, she gifted France large amounts of money to for the restoration of the Versailles Palace.

I recall that on my first visit to Versailles in the 1970s there were several paintings with the notation that they had been generously 'donated' to the French government by Mrs. Post.

While Joseph Urban's Mar-a-Lago was a theatrical tour-de-force bordering on the bizarre, Hillwood was the real thing. It was eclectic and obviously a reflection of Mrs. Post's personal taste but for me it was a revelation. I wanted, rather I needed to learn everything I could about those marvelous objects. It truly opened my eyes to a world I was only beginning to understand and appreciate.

The staff that week at Hillwood was charged with the daily needs of the extended Post household. Her daughters and their families were in residence for the celebrations which took place in venues other than Hillwood. They included a 'private' birthday party for three hundred at the Sulgrave Club and, on her actual birthday the following night, Leon Barzin, her daughter Eleanor's husband, flew to Washington from Paris to conduct the National Symphony Orchestra at Constitution Hall in her honor. Hundreds attended.

As a result of that schedule there were no dinner services at Hillwood and the evenings were free so Gordon and I explored all the interesting dives in Washington.

When the festivities ended, the traveling process was reversed and I, along with the staff members who had made the trip north arrived back at Mar-a-Lago.

A day or so later Mr. Moffat, the Steward called me to his office. He looked up as I entered, smiled, motioned me to sit down and said,

"Well Tom, it's over three months since you came to Mar-a-Lago and I must tell you that we are all extremely pleased with your performance. Mr. Livingston said that you're one of the most agreeable and capable young men he's ever had the pleasure of working with. So, because of his very positive recommendation, I'm inviting you to join us at Hillwood for the Spring season and then on to Camp Topridge for the Summer season."

I didn't know what to say. I never considered 'domestic' work as a permanent profession. I accepted my first position with Mrs. Young because it seemed to be an intriguing summer job and quite frankly, a nineteen-year-old with an uncertain draft status and no degree couldn't find anything better at the time.

When I went to work for the Gardners it was because those aforementioned disqualifications precluded me from finding a good job. My discontent at the Gardners led me to Mar-a-Lago. So I thanked Mr. Moffat for his offer and left his office. He was shocked at my hesitation and I had a difficult decision to make.

Despite the numerous challenges presented by Miss Coffin, my employment at Fairholme was an instructive and reasonably enjoyable experience because of all the amusing interactions I had with 'Madam' herself.

In contrast both Mrs. Gardner and Mrs. Post were inflexibly *old school* in their relationship with their staff – one dared not even attempt to have a straightforward conversation with either one of them. I sometimes felt like a piece of furniture or worse – invisible.

As the 'professional lackey' types retired or expired, there was no one of their mindset to replace them. No young man or woman with an education wanted a career without the possibility of upward mobility. So when a domestic worker arrived at the apogee of his or her ability – they *stayed* there – for the duration of their employment in that particular household. The only way to earn more money in a domestic situation was to quit and find another job in a higher position for a higher salary.

And benefits if any were provided at the discretion and/or generosity of the employer. It was unheard of to be offered medical insurance or a pension. And, to avoid the bother of withholding taxes, etc., salaries were often paid in cash in a little brown envelope.

The next day I informed both Mr. Moffat and Mr. Livingston that while I enjoyed the whole experience of the Post operation, I had reached the decision that I would be 'giving notice' at the end of the season. My reason was that I was now considering staying on in Florida and hoped to find a job in a gallery or a shop.

I did however, request a written Reference. I had learned that one never knew when such a document might come in handy.

Those days Palm Beach shut down when the social season ended. The private beach clubs closed, the Palm Beach Yacht Club at the foot of Worth Avenue held nothing but vacant slips. The shops and restaurants on Worth Avenue had shuttered as did the Royal Poinciana Playhouse and its adjoining boutique complex. Not a soul walked the streets. The was no vehicular traffic, except an occasional, lonely Palm Beach Police patrol car. Nothing would reopen until October.

No one told me that. I should have asked!

I liked Florida. The combination of good weather and the casual attitude toward everyday existence let me to believe that this would be an ideal location to explore my next adventure. It was this mindset that led me to decide to rent an affordable apartment in West Palm Beach and then look for work.

I found a small, furnished bungalow and gave a month's security with the first month's rent. I stocked the larder and the bar feeling I had made the right choice. Wrong! To begin with I should have found a job first, then the apartment. And I was now faced with the realization that, while I had shelter, I had no income and my desire to find a normal nine-to-five job in West Palm Beach was severely hampered by my shaky draft status. And …

If I accepted a job in Florida I was required to change my draft board location to West Palm Beach. As it turned out South Florida and specifically Palm Beach County possessed the highest number of draftees sent to Vietnam. As if that wasn't bad enough, I was told that 'Last in – First out' was the system these boards used to fill their quotas. Since I was still on my New York City draft board list, my task was to get back to the Big Apple as quickly as possible. But I had spent my little 'nest-egg' on the apartment and I couldn't afford to fly back.

But since I finally had something valuable, I decided to use it. I found the only un-shuttered domestic agency in West Palm Beach and showed them my *golden* Reference from Mar-a-Lago. And before I knew it I was southbound for an interview with Mrs. J. Myer Schine in Boca Raton on what else? – another Greyhound bus.

Chapter Five

Hildegarde Schine

My very own Auntie Mame

The bus pulled into a gas station *cum* bus depot on the outskirts of Boca Raton. An older gentleman was waiting. He drove me to a sprawling 1950s house on S.E. Spanish River Road and parked. Then he led me to the poolside entrance of a forty-foot long living room. A woman sat at its far end with her back to me. She was playing a large organ – an instrument so big that it could have been found in a church or movie theater. The music stopped, the woman turned, smiled and said, 'Hello, I'm Hildegarde Schine.'

I approached, introduced myself and somewhat awkwardly showed Mrs. Schine my 'signed-by-Mr.-Moffat' Reference from Mar-a-Lago. She glanced at it and said, "I'm very impressed but I knew the moment I set eyes on you that I liked you – you're hired."

And I liked her! And, to my surprise and delight the salary was significantly more than I earned at Mar-a-Lago.

I had been hired to organize and supervise the closing down and 'mothballing' of the entire twenty-room compound for the coming summer before Mr. and Mrs. Schine flew back to New York for the Spring season. I had three and a half weeks to do this. That accomplished, I was to drive her Rolls Royce, Phantom V limousine packed with her favorite paintings, silver, bronzes and other *objets d'art* to New York. What could have been more perfect? Three more weeks in Florida and then back home where my draft status would be a bit less worrisome.

That afternoon I went back to West Palm Beach on another Greyhound bus, packed my bags, bid good-bye to my landlady and returned to Boca to begin yet another adventure.

Hildegarde's house was filled with an assortment of typical 1950s Florida furniture plus an assemblage of modern sculpture and wall art of the same period. I was not impressed. But then, having recently departed the splendors of Mar-a-Lago and Hillwood, *anyone's* home would pale in comparison.

My lodging however was a pleasant surprise. It consisted of a good size suite with a living room, two bedrooms and a private bath and was nicely furnished with Danish Modern furniture. The quarters were originally intended to house a live-in couple – a Butler and his Housekeeper-wife, but the Schine's unassuming lifestyle didn't mandate the formality I found in my previous positions and so the suite was mine.

With my arrival, the Schine staff swelled to the astounding number of *three*. Yes, three! The two others, Addie and Hyacinth, shared an apartment over the cabanas by the pool.

Unlike my previous locations in Newport and Palm Beach where everyone was white, the Schine's staff was integrated. Addie, the cook was born and grew up in Georgia. Hyacinth, who did *everything* else, was from Jamaica.

In the two weeks before the packing and closing down began, I ran countless errands for Mrs. Shine during the day. However, I had nothing to do in the evenings. So one day I asked if I could begin 'Buttling' and show the others how to properly serve a meal.

She looked at me, giggled, and said,

"Sure, go ahead – and – good luck!"

Hyacinth fought me every step of the way. Her island accent had a timbre that afforded her great success in getting her way more often than not. She would invariably say,

"Oh Thomas, that's too fussy. We don't do all that fancy stuff here."

We eventually made our peace. Hyacinth mellowed and I became less exacting.

Formidable Addie, then in her early fifties was a character out of the movies. Addie was short and stocky and reminded me of Edward G. Robinson. During the Second World War she drove a cement truck during the day and was a short-order cook at night.

Did I mention that she was a chain smoker? Addie was never to be seen without a lit cigarette dangling from her lips or left burning in a nearby ashtray. She also drank.

But she was a real trooper and could handle virtually any situation. For example she was never rattled when Mrs. Schine ordered a poolside lunch for five or six with just half an hour's notice.

Addie was Baptist and attended church every Sunday. As Mrs. Schine allowed us to use any of the cars except her Rolls Royce, Addie's Sunday vehicle of choice was Mr. Schine's Cadillac Fleetwood limousine. One day I asked her why she took that car and she replied,

"Listen here Tom, every time I pull into the church parking lot in that car all the young bucks turn around to see who gets out. I love that!"

Addie was diligent and a fine Southern cook – fried chicken the likes of which you would never find at a restaurant, not to mention her collard greens, grits, pecan pie and, lest we forget, her *sweet* iced tea.

It didn't matter that Addie could create culinary wonders. Mrs. Schine was forever on one diet or another and her husband had simple tastes – broiled chicken or fish with green vegetables and potatoes every night.

Addie however, cooked Southern for herself, for Hyacinth and for me. It took the Irish 'meat-and-potatoes' Tom a while to get used to it, but I ultimately grew to love her cooking.

Being Jewish, Mr. Schine never wanted pork cooked or served in the house. Addie took his directive with a grain of salt and regularly prepared non-kosher meals for herself, Hyacinth and me at lunchtime since he rarely, if ever, had lunch at home. However, when she fried bacon, the kitchen and pantry were thoroughly ventilated before he returned home in the late afternoon.

The couple kept five cars in Boca. There were two limousines – Mrs. Schine's Phantom V Rolls Royce and her husband's silver-grey Cadillac Fleetwood and two convertibles – a Lincoln Continental and a Cadillac Biarritz (her personal car) and an older Buick station-wagon.

I ran countless errands in Mrs. Schine's Biarritz. I traversed Boca endlessly – dropping off or picking up the dry cleaning, buying things at the hardware store or picking up prescriptions at the pharmacy. I made frequent trips to her dressmaker in Del Ray Beach to deliver and/or collect her clothes. I drove forty miles south to the Coconut Grove Bank to cash checks or to the McAllister Hotel in Miami (which they had once owned) to pick up their discounted liquor.

I would no sooner return than there would be 'one more thing' that needed to be done. For example,

"Oh Tom, the florist just called. The flowers are ready but his truck just broke down. Could you please go and pick them up?"

Mrs. Schine was a multitasker. She worked three to five charity and art related projects simultaneously. Her *command center* was on the second floor next to the master bedroom suite. It consisted of her bath/dressing room, a huge walk-in closet and an enclosed sun porch which served as her office. A small elevator gave her access to the ground floor.

Between nine-thirty and ten every morning I was summoned by telephone to her office to pick up my daily schedule. Mrs. Schine depended on telephones. The house had only two phone lines with over twenty extensions. One could answer the phone anywhere on the compound, even poolside, in ten steps or less.

However, the downside of this convenience was that when someone lifted the receiver to make or answer a call, every phone in the entire house lit up indicating that the line was in use. So, when someone made a call after the Schines had retired for the night the lights on the phones on both sides of their king size bed lit up. In moments, Mrs. Schine would pick up her phone and want to know who was on the line and why were they calling at that late hour?

Mrs. Schine's elevator led directly to the swimming pool at ground level. The pool area was often used to entertain the Schine's numerous grandchildren and friends at afternoon gatherings. Occasionally, late at night, Mrs. Schine enjoyed an unannounced skinny-dip so it was understood that no one went near the pool after dark.

Unlike my previous employers, the Schine's allowed their staff to use the pool. I however, was the only one to exploit their generous offer. Addie and Hyacinth had no interest in the pool, day or night.

Mrs. Schine made certain that all the cars were kept in perfect condition. In addition, to the delight of the Boca Raton and Miami body shops, even a minor blemish such as a small dent or a scratch was immediately addressed.

As the days passed my daytime attire became more and more casual since I spent most of my time driving around doing errands. So I, like most young men in Boca, wore a tight tank top, cut-off jeans and a pair of well-worn topsiders.

For the dinner service however, I wore a Brooks Brothers tuxedo that I bought while working for Mrs. Post. I bought it in one of the Palm Beach charity thrift shops where society donates last season's clothes for an annual tax write-off.

It fit me as though it had been custom made. Hyacinth rolled her eyes when she first saw me in it. One evening at dinner, Mrs. Schine commented,

"Tom, you look really handsome in your tuxedo tonight."

Her husband said nothing but gave me a strange look. I was beginning to think he wasn't too happy with my growing rapport with his wife.

He was an early riser and usually breakfasted alone. After he finished, one of his employees would pick him up and drive him to his office, which was roughly two miles from the house. He rarely returned for lunch so I usually saw him only in the evenings.

One Saturday morning he stormed into the pantry grasping a bunch of papers that he literally threw at me, shouting, "What are these?"

I glanced at them and saw that they were bills for cosmetic repairs to the cars. So I answered, "Some are for repairs to Mrs. Schine's limousine and the others are for repairs to yours."

I didn't mention that Addie used his limousine to go to Sunday church services and it was occasionally dented and/or scratched in the church's parking lot.

"It's crazy to waste all this money on those old cars," he shouted.

"I was following Mrs. Schine's instructions. She told me to take the cars in for the repairs."

He tensed up and said in a very angry tone of voice,

"From now on you ask for my approval for any work on the cars first. Do you understand?"

"Sure, Mr. Schine," I answered, and turned to leave.

"Wait!" he barked.

He was seething with anger. Perhaps I hadn't manifested enough deference to his directive. In any case he began to vent his opinion of me.

"You're too friendly with my wife young man – you spend all day together."

"Not true," I thought, "I spend the whole day alone – driving all over Boca and South Florida doing her errands."

"And another thing, I don't like how you dress around my wife – that sleeveless shirt and those short-shorts of yours are indecent. And you're too bossy with Addie and Hyacinth. Just let them do their jobs. Watch your step young man!"

And with that last admonishment he stormed out of the room.

He was wrong about my relationship with Addie and Hyacinth. I had bonded with both of them and they had grown quite fond of me. They no longer referred to me as, "That snobby guy from Palm Beach."

He must have given the same directive to Mrs. Schine because she stopped having the dents or scratches repaired in Boca. But, true to her good and generous nature she never rescinded her permission for Addie and me to use any of the cars except the Rolls.

Several days passed. I kept busy with her perpetual errands and closing down the house. The house continued to be the venue for small poolside gatherings and dinners for family and friends. Soon I began packing for the trip north. All was running smoothly until …

One evening I had set the table for dinner, placed the fresh flowers and donned my tuxedo that was just back from the cleaners, when Addie gave me the sign that she was ready to start. I entered the living room and announced dinner. It would be their usual boring meal – a tiny salad, followed by grilled fish, green beans and some boiled potatoes.

They entered the dining room. I stood behind Mrs. Schine's chair and assisted her as she sat. Mr. Schine made his way to his chair, plopped down noisily, and glared at me when Mrs. Schine commented once again as to how especially nice I looked that evening.

When they finished their salads, I cleared the plates and replaced them with two warmed dinner plates. But I sensed a curious 'vibe' in the room. Something was about to happen and I didn't know what.

As usual Addie placed the entire main course on a large three-sectioned silver platter – a good idea for offering the main course as it permitted the chicken or fish, the green vegetable and the potatoes to be served together. Less work for Thomas!

I served Mrs. Schine first and when I went over to Mr. Schine to offer him his dinner, he mumbled something about his displeasure with the time I spent with his wife and my revolting attire while doing so, and …

Without warning he pushed the food-laden platter up and onto my chest with an animated move. The chicken, green beans, potatoes and gravy landed – on the table, on the floor and – on me.

"MYER!" Mrs. Schine shouted.

Once I regained my wits, I thought, "What would Livingston do?"

So I assessed the damage to the table, the china, the stemware, the carpet and me, looked at Mrs. Schine and said, "Good night Mrs. Schine."

As I walked through the pantry I stopped momentarily and asked Hyacinth to go in and see what she could do. Then I went back to my room, took off my soiled tuxedo, showered, put on my jeans, an Izod, my topsiders, went to the garage, got in the Buick station-wagon and headed out – not knowing what the outcome of the bizarre events might be.

The following morning, reviewing the previous evening's drama, I thought to myself, "How could he do something like that? He must be insane!"

I didn't want to quit – I really liked Mrs. Schine and Addie and Hyacinth were easy to work with. More importantly, I wanted to go back to New York. I didn't want to be stranded in Boca.

When I walked into the pantry Addie and Hyacinth couldn't hide their admiration and amusement. Addie gave me a big smile. So I poured my first cup of coffee and asked her for scrambled eggs and toast. It was clear that no one had ever gotten the upper hand when dealing with Mr. Schine in a head-on confrontation.

Once I finished breakfast, Addie told me that Mrs. Schine wanted to see me in her office.

I arrived at the door to her office, knocked and entered. She looked up and smiled broadly. Whether she was amused by her husband's jealousy or simply the craziness of the event itself, I'll never know for certain. Then she said calmly,

"Please sit down Tom."

"I really want to apologize for my husband's conduct last night. I don't know what's gotten into him. He's never done anything like that before."

So I said,

"Mrs. Schine, I'm not certain I can continue working here after last night."

"Don't say that Tom. My husband seems to have gotten a bee in his bonnet about your sleeveless shirt and those cut-off jeans. So, let's make a deal. You stop wearing the shirt and jeans and I'll have him apologize for his inexcusable behavior last night"

"Ok," I said relieved and smiling, "It's a deal."

That afternoon I went to Mr. Schine's office. His secretary escorted me in. He was seated behind his desk. He looked at me and the self-made, multi-millionaire apologized to the twenty-year-old kid who worked for him and his wife.

(Junius) Myer Schine was born in Latvia in 1890. In 1902, fleeing the poverty and anti-Semitism of late-nineteenth century Eastern Europe, J. Myer, his mother and younger brother, Louis, joined their father in Jamestown, New York. (It was not unusual for male family members to emigrate first and send for the others after they had established themselves.)

The ambitious brothers, seeking greater economic opportunity, learned English quickly and worked at various humble jobs in the Jamestown and Buffalo area.

They labored in a local mill and cut and sold candy on passenger trains. Later J. Myer worked in a clothing store while Louis worked at a newsstand in the train station. When the First World War began, Louis enlisted in the army.

By 1914 J. Myer accumulated enough money to start his own business. He bought an interest in the Novelty Theater – a dingy nickelodeon in Syracuse.

In 1917 he sold his share of the Novelty and bought the Hippodrome Theater in Gloversville, a factory town that manufactured – gloves.

Continuing in his frugal ways J. Meyer resided at the YMCA for three years. When Louis returned from the war he joined the business. By 1920 the brothers added the Glove Theatre in Gloversville and converted it to a vaudeville house.

Business flourished and J. Myer moved out of the YMCA and relocated to the Kingsborough, an upscale hotel.

Beautiful and talented Hildegarde Frances Feldman was born in 1903 in Johnstown, New York where her parents owned a thriving furniture business. She studied voice and piano at 'The Castle,' a music conservatory in Tarrytown.

When she graduated Johnstown High School she began to give music lessons. On her eighteenth birthday she went on her first date with J. Myer and four years later, they married.

Expanding their theatrical empire in the 1920s the Schine brothers purchased the Lyceum Theater in Amsterdam, New York (and renamed it the Mohawk) and the Strand Theater in Oneonta, New York. Over the next nine years they increased their theatrical holdings to one hundred and fifty theaters.

In 1929, when talkies were revolutionizing the movie industry, the bigger Hollywood studios decided to create movie theater chains of their own. The Fox Theater Corporation purchased ninety-eight theaters from the Schine brothers for top dollar – just before the stock market crash.

Cash rich in a depressed economy, the Schines began buying up valuable properties including hotels at bargain basement prices. By the late 1940s they owned and managed hotels such as the Ritz-Carlton in Atlantic City, New Jersey, the Ten Eyck Hotel in Albany, New York, the Hotel Northampton and the Wiggins Tavern in Northampton, Massachusetts and the Breakwater Court Hotel in Kennebunkport, Maine. In Florida they owned the Boca Raton Club in Boca Raton, the Roney Plaza Hotel on Miami Beach and the McAllister Hotel in downtown Miami. In Los Angeles they owned the Ambassador Hotel – home of the famous Brown Derby.

By 1965 the Schines holdings, accumulated over a forty-eight year period, consisted of sixty motion picture theatres, three thousand acres of oceanfront land in Palm Beach and Boca Raton and twelve hotels. The properties had an estimated value of one hundred and fifty million dollars and were sold to real estate partners, Lawrence Wien and Harry Helmsly for an undisclosed amount.

Having resolved what seemed to be a hopeless situation, Mrs. Schine was so delighted with her ability as peacemaker that she instructed me to immediately go to the Lilly Pulitzer boutique in downtown Boca and buy myself a complete new ensemble on her charge account. Within the hour, I bought a pair of Lilly's lion's-head-motif sail-cloth pants, a matching belt, the best pair of Top-Siders they had, and an almost see-through, coral-pink silk shirt.

Closing down the house proceeded apace. The Schines planned to fly up to New York and Addie, accompanied by Hyacinth would drive the Caddy limousine and I would drive the Rolls. Addie said she enjoyed ferrying the Schine cars back and forth between Boca and New York.

Both vehicles were filled to the maximum with Mrs. Schine's silver, paintings, bronzes, *objets d'art* – in addition to her clothing bags and suitcases packed with formal evening wear, gowns, furs and shoes for the Spring season in New York.

I told Mrs. Schine that anyone glancing through the side windows would realize that there was a treasure trove just waiting to be stolen in these two very visible luxury cars. I explained that not only would we be making many stops for food and gas but also that Addie and I would have at least one overnight stop in a motel. So I suggested that our 'cargo' should somehow be concealed.

In a flash Mrs. Schine had the solution. She dashed up to one of the closets in her dressing room and returned with a huge chinchilla throw that must have cost a fortune. Its back had a dark lining so I reversed it and concealed the Rolls contents with it. Pragmatic Addie just threw a bed sheet over the contents of the Cadillac.

The Schines hired local Boca men to drive the other cars directly to Myhil (an acronym for Myer and Hildegarde), their summer compound west of Albany in upper New York State. The Schines provided the drivers with airline tickets to fly back to Florida from Albany.

I learned something disturbing about the United States on that drive up to New York. The Interstate Highway System, I-95 was not yet finished so drivers were obliged use old Route 301 in Georgia and South Carolina.

The 'Whites-Only' signs at many restaurants and motels made me realize that an era I had only heard and read about was still alive and well. The just-over-two-year-old Civil Rights Act of 1964 was clearly being ignored in the 'Old South.'

I was upset. Why should I be able to eat and sleep anywhere I liked while my friends and co-workers Addie and Hyacinth were obliged to find a place that accepted black people? When we stopped for gas I vocalized my distress. Addie said, 'Don't be bothered Tom. Change is always slow.'

I called my parents after we arrived in New York. My mother told me that several of my high-school buddies had been inducted into the Army and were on their way to Vietnam. I was certain my time was coming. I told that to Mrs. Schine and she graciously suggested that I stay in her employ until the fateful day when my letter of 'Greetings' from Uncle Sam arrived.

The Schines lived at Four East Sixty Sixth Street – a limestone-faced, Italian Renaissance-style apartment building designed by J.E.R. Carpenter, one of New York City's finest residential architects. The twelve-story structure was completed in 1920 and stands on Fifth Avenue facing Central Park and abutting Temple Emanu-El.

Four East was a 'white glove building' with twenty-four hour doormen and elevator operators. The doormen's uniforms included white gloves, or at least they did in my time, hence that appellation. It offered all the services that one would expect from a building with such an impressive address.

Each apartment occupied an entire floor with the living room and the library facing Central Park. The Schines redesigned part of the apartment to create an extremely large bedroom suite with 'His' and 'Hers' bath and dressing rooms. The apartment was dramatically furnished in a pseudo-French Louis XV style.

One of the remaining bedroom suites was reserved for guests. The other was occupied by C. Richard Schine, their younger son. Richard was in his late thirties and divorced. He was father to two young boys who lived with their mother.

The 'back' of the apartment held the Butler's pantry, a state of the art kitchen, the staff dining room and five small staff bedrooms. Two of those bedrooms had been combined to house a huge central air conditioning unit. A third was the office of Mrs. Stein, Mrs. Schine's personal secretary. Addie and Hyacinth occupied the remaining two staff bedrooms.

The living room, library, dining room and bedroom suites occupied the 'front' of the apartment. All of them had functioning wood-burning fireplaces. But since it was late April and temperatures were rising quickly all of them had been cleaned and filled with decorative white birch logs – with one exception.

C. Richard burned logs in his fireplace every night – even on the warmest spring evenings so firewood was piled high in both his bedroom and in the vestibule near the service elevator.

The central air conditioning unit was challenged by the heat from his fireplace and so the largest air conditioning window unit available at that time had been installed in his room.

Life at Four East was notably calmer and easier than in Boca. Mrs. Stein did much of the work I had done for Mrs. Schine in Florida. And I was now a full-time Butler/chauffeur working in an elegant Fifth Avenue apartment in New York City. However – there was no room for me in their crowded apartment.

Mrs. Schine said I could use the guest bedroom suite when it wasn't needed. I was certain however, that Mr. Schine wouldn't embrace the idea of *me* living in the bedroom suite normally reserved for family and becoming a permanent part of his New York household. So I formulated another solution and suggested that every evening after my workday was done, I would take one of their cars and drive to my parents' home in Bayside, Queens for the night.

Mrs. Schine thought it was a great idea and so when I asked if I could use the Rolls she said, "Sure."

So most evenings after finishing my duties I would take the Rolls from the garage on East Sixty-seventh Street and drive home to Queens. On rare evenings when the Schines attended a private dinner party, a Broadway show or a function at Lincoln Center, I would drive them to the given location, return to collect them, then take them back home before driving the Rolls to my parents' house.

On those warm spring evenings I took the long way home and stopped at the local White Castle just off Queens Boulevard for a snack. The reaction of the other patrons as the Phantom V Rolls Royce glided into the White Castle's parking lot was one of total amazement. I just loved it!

Despite the fact that my parents lived in a secure, middle-class neighborhood, my New-York-City-police-detective-father had great misgivings concerning the overnight stay of the Rolls. You see, with the added six-inches in height for the 'opera' light on its roof – the Rolls was too high to fit into the garage. It was also too long – five feet too long.

So the only solution was to leave it outside on the driveway. The next morning everyone in the neighborhood knew that Tom Gardner was obviously employed by an enormously wealthy family.

The Schines came from the Johnstown-Gloversville area of upstate New York. Years before the Schines had purchased the two hundred and twenty acres across the road from Caroga Lake for Myhil, their summer home. They always scheduled their drive to Myhil to coincide with the Gloversville Bank's annual picnic.

Mrs. Schine, as was often the case, asked her son C. Richard to help her select the proper attire for the picnic. The dialogue took place in Mrs. Schine's dressing room at Four East with both Hyacinth and me in attendance.

C. Richard rose to the challenge. From a clothing rack he took two wonderful Emilio Pucci pants suits and asked his mother to select one. Then he pulled several Channel scarves from an open drawer and did the same. Next came an elegant Saks Fifth Avenue silk blouse and a pair of black patent leather Gucci boots and a large sun hat. He finished off her outfit with a selection of long gold chains encrusted with semi-precious stones.

That done, he told his mother how wonderful she'll look exiting the Rolls Royce limousine in the middle of a cow pasture.

Hyacinth and I just looked at each other and raised our eyebrows.

C. Richard also articulated his hope that there wouldn't be any serious rainfall the evening before the picnic because the Rolls Royce was quite heavy and the muddy 'cow' pasture would present a problem. They therefore discussed which of the other four vehicles was up to the task.

In addition to the cars that Addie and I drove up, the Schines had two more that were kept in New York – a new four-door Mercedes and C. Richard's customized Oldsmobile Toronado.

The solution was obvious. C. Richard needed his car in the city and the Mercedes was too small so Mr. Schine's Cadillac Fleetwood limousine was readied for the trip and the Rolls stayed in New York.

The next morning I drove the Schines and Addie to Gloversville. The picnic did *not* take place in a cow pasture but at the local fair-grounds outside of town. C. Richard had apparently angered the gods with his bad jesting because the night before the picnic it not only rained in Gloversville – it poured.

We arrived the Fair Grounds and drove onto the muddy field. As we left the stability of the paved County Road and drove onto the open field, I began to worry – the limousine seemed to be sinking into the soft mud. However, when we four alighted, it stabilized. Whew!

The picnickers showered the Schines with good wishes, smiles and handshakes. It was an interesting experience. I witnessed and appreciated the positive interaction between them and the people of Gloversville – many of whom worked or had worked for them. In many ways all those present from the youngest to the oldest had a direct connection to them.

They were Rock Stars that day.

We stayed about an hour and then drove on to Myhil. Years before the Schines purchased two hundred and twenty acres of land across the road from Caroga Lake for their summer place. By 1967 Myhil had expanded to a large compound with their house at its center. Over the years the house had grown larger and larger with Mrs. Shine's extensions.

The garage was big enough to accommodate the numerous vehicles that were on hand when the Schine's were in residence. There, the Cadillac Biarritz and the Lincoln convertible that had recently been driven up from Boca were joined by a new Mercury station-wagon.

Housed in a separate building was a private movie theater seating fifteen. Mr. Schine's movie industry connections provided all the current films and a local Gloversville projectionist showed them to us twice weekly.

The compound's jewel was the stable. It was designed by C. Richard Schine himself and reminded me of a Swiss chalet. C. Richard's building venture demonstrated his expensive taste. Great care went into its construction especially in the detailed woodwork. There were no horses stabled that summer since there were no riders in residence. I believe that the horses were hired if and when the need arose.

Mr. Schine would frequently commute between New York and Myhil. After lunch I would drive him to the Albany airport for the afternoon Mohawk airlines flight to the city. Since Mrs. Schine had both a local family-retainer cook and a maid at Myhil, Hyacinth stayed in New York to attend to C. Richard and Mr. Schine's needs.

Mrs. Schine enjoyed the simple, low pressure country lifestyle. So our life at Myhil was extremely casual and had no fixed routine. The area however, was a densely-populated summer community with the predictable congestion and so driving was nightmarish and we stayed on the compound most of the time.

Mrs. Schine staged several small dinner parties for a select group of old friends and family. I really enjoyed them since they gave me the opportunity to display my Buttling expertise and, of course, Mrs. Schine enjoyed showing me off that way. It was fun for me and she and her guests enjoyed it.

That summer I developed an intestinal blockage of some sort. At first, I paid it no serious attention – with the insouciance of youth I thought it would just run its course. But a few days later I began to experience great pain and discomfort. Mrs. Schine took command. She made one phone call and then drove me to Gloversville to be seen by her own family physician – the same man who delivered her children. The next morning I was in surgery in the Gloversville Hospital.

After leaving the I.C.U. the next afternoon I was wheeled into my private room. To my amazement I saw my parents standing inside with Mrs. Schine at their side. She notified them of my situation and they had driven up that morning.

Mrs. Schine brought, I swear, a gallon of homemade chicken soup to speed my recovery – and that generous lady paid my entire Hospital bill.

After my discharge I spent several days at Myhil slowly recovering my strength. Addie prepared gallons of chicken soup. Then my parents decided I should finish recuperating at home. Two days later they drove back to Myhil and took me home.

I registered for the Draft at my local draft board on Main Street in Flushing, New York shortly after my eighteenth birthday. I was accompanied by my father who was then serving as a New York City Detective. His presence was to lend me moral support as I had decided to register as a C.O. – a Conscientious Objector. I didn't object for religious reasons – I always had ethical and moral problems with war and killing. However, I was still eligible for the Draft.

When I dropped out of the Collegiate Business Institute in 1966 my student deferment from the Draft terminated. All the state and local draft boards employed a quota system under which they selected men between eighteen and twenty-six to be the drafted into the Armed Forces. No one knew when they might be called up so it was difficult to make any long-term plans. It was a nerve-wracking period for all involved.

I was at my parents' home continuing my post-operation recovery when my 'ORDER TO REPORT FOR INDUCTION' arrived. The instructions were simple and clear – I was instructed to report to my local draft board and be prepared to 'NOT RETURN HOME.' My parents were of the opinion that due to my recent surgery, I would be granted a deferment for several months. That didn't happen.

I called Mrs. Schine and told her I would not be returning to Myhil. She wished me well and asked me to stay in contact with her.

Chapter Six

A Military Interlude

When I entered my draft board office I joined a group of twenty young men. We were bussed to the Fort Hamilton Army Base at the foot of the Verrazano-Narrows Bridge in Brooklyn. There we underwent both physical and psychological examinations. All 'passed' and were immediately sworn into the Army. Then we were bussed to Kennedy airport where we boarded a non-military plane to Columbia Metropolitan Airport near Fort Jackson, South Carolina where Basic Training would begin.

I was put in charge of making sure that every new soldier found his way onto the flight as I was the oldest and appeared to be the most capable of controlling the group. We arrived in the darkest hours of the early morning and were bussed to the base where we were processed. That experience should happen just once in one's lifetime. After a host of inoculations, our hair was cut short – and we were issued Army fatigues and our Class-A dress uniforms. Then they fed us (for the first time) before testing our ability to interpret Morse code. Everyone failed.

Later that day, realizing that I had been inducted as a C.O. and was therefore not required to have weapons training, I found myself on yet a second flight – this time to Fort Sam Houston in San Antonio. 'Fort Sam' was the only Basic Training location for C.O.s. The Army, out of all the branches of the Armed Forces, was the only one that accepted C.O.s

Basic Training was a rough routine. We were roused at five-thirty in the morning, showered and prepared our barracks for its daily inspection. After breakfast in the mess hall we returned to our barracks to receive our orders for that day. We learned to march and were given insight into the meaning of the 'Military Code of Justice,' which itemized the infractions that could lead to a court-marshal.

At the time C.O.s were given the limited choice of becoming a cook or a medic. I chose to be an Army Combat Medic.

At the end of Basic Training, I was given the opportunity to opt into a two-week *Leadership Cadet Training (LCT)* course. The goal of the two-week course was to enable us to improve each soldier's ability to understand an order and to carry it out – no matter what their personal opinion of its value or validity was.

I accepted, and after completing my Basic Training I became an *acting* Corporal, a Non-Commissioned-Officer (N.C.O.) who would supervise the other 'medics-to-be' in the *Advanced Individual Training (AIT)* courses to come.

Three others from my C.O. group were accepted and we moved to a new set of barracks across the street. Except for myself and the two other C.O.s – the remaining twenty-seven others were all regular, weapons-trained Army.

To distinguish N.C.O.s from everyone else our helmets were not regulation green but a high-gloss purple – we were therefore referred to as 'Grape-Heads.'

Taking on responsibilities of an N.C.O. Corporal afforded me a daily 'over-night' pass. San Antonio proved to be quite a town and despite the fact that I had to be back at base very early, its night life was magical.

In the *Advanced Individual Training* we learned all the skills required of an Army Combat Medic. When I graduated this course I could do everything from running a morning sick call to treating the most severe battlefield injuries. If the casualties can survive a battlefield injury until they reached the combat support hospital, aka MASH, their survival rate can reach 98%.

We practiced and perfected our skills on human-patient simulators. We learned to apply a tourniquet, insert an IV, and dress severe battlefield wounds. We were given a final test which I, and most of the others passed.

Throughout this ordeal I corresponded regularly with my former employer, Hildegarde Schine. I found it comforting to imagine her typing those very personal, warm and supportive letters to me on her turquoise Smith-Corona portable typewriter.

The policy at Fort Sam was to close down for Christmas. Therefore, everyone was 'On Leave' and could go home for the holiday if they wished or spend their leave in San Antonio. The Vietnam war was raging and so all the potential Medics had come to grips with the strong possibility of being sent to Vietnam. So going home might be the last time we saw our families – or they us.

A few days before I went home for the holiday, I was ordered to report to the Headquarters of my Commanding officer, Colonel Charles Calvin Pixley in my Class-A dress uniform. It was a very hot day and I was obliged to walk at least a mile from my barracks to Headquarters.

When I arrived, I was soaking wet from heat and anxiety. I was ordered to wait in the anti-room to the Colonel's office. A short time later, I was instructed to, "Knock, then enter," and I did, with great trepidation.

At the far end of the room, seated at a large Army-issue desk, was Colonel Pixley. After the formal salutes were exchanged, he all but shouted,

"AT EASE, PRIVATE GARDNER!"

He stared at me with obvious disapproval and then removed a letter from a folder on his desk. His next words I not only remember verbatim but also will take to my grave. He looked down at the letter, then asked in his very loud voice,

"PRIVATE GARDNER," *pause*, "DO YOU KNOW" *pause*, "AND HAVE YOU HAD RECENT CORRESPONDENCE WITH" *pause*, "A WOMAN BY THE NAME OF" *very long pause*, "MRS. J. MYER SCHINE?"

"Yes sir," I replied – as unsettling thoughts raced through my mind, "Oh my God! What has she done now?" Followed by, "I'm going to spend the rest of my life in Leavenworth," or worse yet, "I'm going to be shot."

The Colonel posed a few other questions regarding my father, the people I had worked for and my organizational ability. Having satisfactorily answered, the Colonel simply said,

"DISMISSED PRIVATE GARDNER," and I left, mystified.

Mrs. Schine sent me a carbon copy of the letter she sent to Colonel Pixley. I received it two days after the frightening interview. It stated that she had heard that Colonel Pixley was looking for a 'chauffeur,' and she was recommending me for the job. She dropped names and places and mentioned that my father was a *leading* New York detective. I realized that if the Colonel hired me as his chauffeur, I would remain at Fort Sam for the rest of my tour. Therefore, *no* Vietnam.

That was my beloved Hildegarde Schine's plan. It didn't work.

When I returned to Fort Sam after Christmas leave I learned that I was assigned to the First and Thirty-Sixth Armored Division, a Howitzer Unit in West Germany. That made my parents very happy. Me too!

On a cold January morning I landed at the Rhine/Main Air Base in Frankfurt am Main. Confusion reigned in Frankfurt where everyone on the plane was bound for a different location. I eventually boarded the train to the historic town of Ulm, which had been bombed significantly in the Second World War.

Ulm was the birthplace of Albert Einstein and its ancient Münster still has the tallest church spire in the World. The church survived the bombing with just minor damage. I was making my way to my post at the Wiley Kaserne in the Bavarian town of Neu-Ulm on the opposite bank of the River Danube.

My touch-typing ability that I learned in my year at the Collegiate Business Institute in New York made me the keeper of medical records of all the soldiers in my unit and their families. My organizational ability impressed not only my immediate superiors but also the Captain and Field Grade Officer doctors who relied on those files to make evaluations of any given patient. Within a month, three assistants were answerable to me. This in turn afforded me a daily overnight pass – but Ulm unfortunately, was no San Antonio.

While there, I assisted two mothers in the delivery of their babies in my dispensary where, if necessary, emergency medical aid was provided 24/7.

In the Spring my unit was given its 'Marching Orders.' We were to be relocated to the much larger Bavarian city of Augsburg. This move necessitated an unbelievable act of coordination by both road and rail. There were three eight-inch Howitzer tank Batteries – Companies A, B and C and the Headquarters. But in true military form, 'Orders Given – Orders Carried Out.'

I was stationed in Reese Barracks which had been part of a Wehrmacht Kaserne built in the late 1930s for the German Heer (Army) and Luftwaffe (Airforce) in the ponderous 19th-century German Military style.

Bavaria in southern Germany has three major cities – Stuttgart, Augsburg and München (Munich). Each has its own outstanding characteristics – but for me, Munich held the greatest allure. It appeared that, for one reason or another, the city was forever partying – Octoberfest, Fasching (Karneval), Christmas, New Year – and when one of their sports teams won a match. Munich was half an hour's train ride from Augsburg – and that made it even more attractive.

Our unit's annual 'field maneuvers' were to take place in Gräfenburg – a town northeast of Nuremburg. It had once been the training area for Heinrich Himmler's *SS*. For me it is the most desolate and depressing region in all Germany because it was there that fate presented me with a life-changing event whose tragic memory I still bear today.

My duty, along with my Medic partner Paul's, was to be on call at the 'field maneuvers' in the event of an accident. We waited for the dreaded call in our unit's 'Cracker Box,' that is, our ambulance.

When our 'move-out' orders arrived on that cold and dark March morning, Howitzer Battery 'A' – consisting of four, self-propelled, eight inch M110 Howitzers (the Army's largest cannon) began to move to a specified location to 'dig-in' – that is, ram the Howitzer's massive hydraulic rear 'recoil spade' into the frozen ground to absorb the powerful recoil following the Howitzer's firing.

Paul and I were several hundred yards from the four Howitzers which were in the digging-in process in preparation for firing when the ominous call came over our ambulance radio,

'Two men down – Immediate aid needed!' In a split second we were on our way. We arrived at a scene of utter chaos. A cluster of at least a half dozen men encircled a man who turned out to be the Sargent Major of Battery 'A.' A few feet to the side another soldier – a Corporal, was also on the ground. Both were severely injured.

It was apparent what had happened. Two Howitzers, while attempting to position themselves into firing position had accidently backed into each other with their 'recoil spades' in the upright position. Unaware that the Howitzers were making their final adjustments prior to digging-in, the Corporal and the Sargent Major were crushed between them.

The Corporal survived – the Sargent Major died in my arms.

Chapter Seven

Hilles Timpson

Lazy summer days and marvelous nights

In the summer of 1969 I received an Honorable Discharge and came back to the States. My mother picked me up at Fort Dix on August 21st and as we drove home she said,

"Tom, your father and I believe you should start college now – it's now or never. You're eligible for the GI Bill and we both think you should take advantage of it. You can live at home. You'll have no expenses."

I agreed. I was twenty-three years old and the time *had* come. While I was in West Germany, I enrolled in the University of Maryland college courses the Army offered – so my entrance into college would take place easily without even having to take an entrance exam.

But it was too late to matriculate for the upcoming fall term at St. John's University – my college of choice – so I decided to find another domestic position for six months or a year. With my qualifications and References, I could earn a lot more money than at any other temporary job.

With this in mind who better to call than Mrs. Schine? When I phoned her, she told me that she and her husband were uncertain of their plans regarding the upcoming Winter season because she hadn't been feeling well and was spending long periods of time at health spas. She added that Mr. Schine, living a Spartan lifestyle in their New York apartment, was moodier than ever.

I thought about my rise in status in less than a year and a half. I had risen from lowly houseman to Butler with significant increases in salary with each new position. So I decided to once again hit the Madison Avenue agencies – this time I chose the 'Hedlend.'

In order to give the impression that their clients were all of Social Register level the entire staff at Hedland was exceedingly patronizing and therefore any applicant was fortunate to even be considered for a position with one of 'their' families.

I was tanned and toned from my two years in the Army and still quite young, so when I applied for the position of Butler – their reception was frigid to say the least. But when I showed them my two impressive References – the first from Frank Moffat at Mar-a-Lago and the other from Mrs. Schine – their attitude instantly changed.

I decided to be a bit more demanding in my requirements when accepting a new position. They were:

1. My quarters must have a private bathroom with a shower.

2. In addition to my day off I wanted time off every Sunday to attend church.

3. The staff car or another house vehicle was to be made available to me for my free evenings.

4. If the given location was in an apartment house, I would *not* be required to use the service entrance or the service elevator or the back stairs as my means of exit or entry.

Last, and most important:

5. Employer-paid medical insurance.

The 'Hedlend' ladies were shocked by my demands. But I had already worked in wealthy homes where the staff's future was disregarded. For example, at Mrs. Young's or the Gardner's or even at Mrs. Post's there was no chance of advancement and no health or pension benefits. So I decided to make a point and to my surprise and delight – they accepted.

Bob Dylan was right – 'The Times They Are A-Changin.'

My interview with Mrs. Robert Clermont Livingston was at the agency. The position was Butler/valet at the Marshlands, the Timpson's estate in Southampton, Long Island. The end of the Summer season was fast approaching and so the job would last for about six weeks. So the Headland prorated my commission to just one weeks salary.

Mrs. Timpson agreed to my requirements and hired me. I decided to take the job for three reasons – it was in the Hamptons so I could easily visit New York on my time off – the salary was unusually high – and perhaps most importantly – a reference from the socially-prominent couple (Mrs. Timpson was a Fish-Morris and Mr. Timpson, an Astor) would be invaluable when added to my two 'golden' References when I started job interviews for the rapidly approaching Palm Beach Winter season.

Descended from the Dutch and British founding families of New York, Hilles Morris Timpson was the daughter of Elizabeth Miles Wynkoop and Stuyvesant Fish Morris, Jr. She was a direct descendant of Martin Van Buren, the eighth president of the United States and of a signer of the American Declaration of Independence, Louis Morris. She was born in Quogue, Long Island in 1907.

Her third husband, Robert Claremont Livingston Timpson was an Astor on his mother's side and was also descended from New York's founding families and owned an eponymous New York brokerage firm. He was born in Kloof (near Durban), KwaZulu Natal, South Africa in 1908.

I arrived in Southampton on the Long Island Rail Road and was met by Mr. Roland, the Timpson's former Butler. He was driving a British-racing-green Ford pick-up truck with the logo 'Marshlands' in gold leaf on both doors. Mr. Roland had recently been elevated to the position of Steward at The Marshlands. (Hence the need for a replacement – me.)

The trip from the train station to the house took about ten minutes. Since there were no gates to the estate, two giant, hundred-year-old oaks linked with a heavy sea-anchor chain safeguarded the entrance to The Marshlands.

The chain was always down when the Timpson's were in residence. We drove between the trees and down a serpentine drive to the house. Walls of rhododendron towered above us. Gaps revealed manicured lawns of Kentucky blue grass. It was quite beautiful.

Hilles Morris married her first husband, tobacco heir and sportsman, Louis Gordon Hamersley in October 1926. The couple had three sons and a daughter. Mr. Hamersley was a speedboat enthusiast. The speedboat Mercury was built for him and launched the year he married Hilles. The family's principal residence at that time was in Tuxedo Park, New York but they also built 'The Marshlands,' a thirty-acre summer compound in Southampton on Eastern Long Island. The compound had a sixteen-hundred-foot frontage on Great Peconic Bay.

On the main floor of the three-story main house was the entrance hall and the living room with a porch overlooking Ram Island. Bedrooms were on the second and third floors. The house was elegantly furnished with American and English antiques. On the east side of the main house was an attached two-story structure with two boat slips on the first floor and the so-called 'Great Room' with its open deck facing the Great Peconic Bay on the second. The long pier extending into the Bay was nearby.

Over the years the summer residence had grown to accommodate the needs of the family. A large, two-story structure connected to the main house by a covered breezeway was added to the complex. The kitchen and staff dining room were on the ground level and the Butler's pantry and formal dining room were on the upper level. A 'dumb-waiter' linked the kitchen and the pantry.

Five years after her first husband's death in 1942, Hilles Hamersley married George Lesley Bartlett, her second husband. Mr. Robert Timpson was her third and last husband. There were no children born to either her second or third marriages.

The Timpsons were out when I arrived with Mr. Roland. He showed me to my quarters on the first floor of the main house, then asked me to join him in the staff dining room to meet the other staff members.

My quarters had the 'private bathroom with a shower' that I had demanded. I unpacked quickly, took a quick shower and changed into my clothes since I would not be on duty until the following morning. Then I walked across the breezeway into the staff dining room.

Gathered around the table, enjoying their afternoon tea break, were my fellow staff members. It was a small group but I saw at first glance that they were all old-school domestics. Uh-oh!

By the shocked looks on their faces when they saw me I knew what they were thinking – 'He's too young to be a Butler,' or 'He's an American – the Butler in a house like this should be English.'

Had they known of my past employment working as a Junior Butler at Mar-a-Lago and at Hillwood they might have changed their tune – or perhaps not. No matter what the judgments of the other staff members (of me) would be, this reality followed me for several years – especially from those I classified as 'professional lackeys.' Just Molly the cook who I later discovered was also starting out with the Timpsons, smiled at me and winked.

I met Mr. Timpson for the first time in the Great Room. He was a strikingly handsome man – at least six-foot-four with a full head of steel-grey hair. Although an American, Mr. Timpson had the bearing of a British aristocrat.

Before and after the Southampton season the Timpsons spent a few weeks in London before returning to their home in Kloof, KwaZulu Natal, South Africa, Mr. Timpson's birthplace.

I soon learned that addressing a Butler or a former Butler by his surname was inexcusable. I should have been aware of this since at Mrs. Post's no one ever addressed 'Mr. Livingston,' the Butler as 'Livingston.' But, with no slight intended, I made the deplorable mistake of calling the new Steward and former Butler, 'Roland.'

Being both British and 'old school,' he couldn't deal with my intolerable infraction of this unwritten rule. Within hours he complained to Mrs. Timpson of my ignorant behavior. So, after she enlightened me with a hard-to-conceal smile, I made a grand gesture and began calling him, 'Mr. Roland.'

Oddly enough one of the most inflexible hierarchies surviving among the 'old school' staff members was the manner in which they wished to be addressed. At that time their traditions were more rigid than those of their employers who, on account of their up-bringing and education, had been exposed to a more tolerant view of the human experience and adapted to the times.

The Timpsons were not socially active in Southampton. They regarded their stay as purely recreational and staged no formal receptions or dinner parties. They had no houseguests except for an occasional visit from Mrs. Timpson's children from her first marriage and their offspring.

However, even when alone the Timpsons dressed for dinner. They started each evening with a cocktail hour in the Great Room, then sauntered slowly over the breezeway to the dining room.

Mrs. Timpson had a 1930s movie-star figure and always wore one of her Emilio Pucci floor-length silk gowns and one thoughtfully-chosen piece of jewelry. Mr. Timpson wore his bespoke, deep-blue velour, formal dinner jacket with satin lapels. They were both magnificent.

They sat at opposite ends of the dining table – just as Mrs. Young had allowed the duke and duchess to do at Fairholme. However, the Timpson's table wasn't as long as Mrs. Young's, so a quiet conversation was possible. After dinner they went back to the Great Room and relaxed with coffee and an after-dinner chat for about an hour.

The Timpsons were delighted with my formal dinner service. My ability to provide such a polished technique was due to the meticulous training I had had with Mrs. Young at Fairholme. Her 'Butler-in-Training' lessons were almost as grueling as my Basic Training in the Army.

Even on hot, humid summer evenings the Timpsons walked back to the Great Room for their after dinner coffee. More often than not, Mrs. Timpson would light a fire. It was atmospheric but necessitated the cleaning and re-laying the fireplace the next morning in preparation for the next evening's repeat performance.

Because the Marshlands is located on a salt-water marsh off Long Island Sound, it is the habitat of millions upon millions of small flying and crawling insects. Included in this mixture are the tiniest of flies called 'nits' that are attracted to any and every source of light. They could enter effortlessly into the Great Room through the wire-mesh window screens.

When the after-dinner coffee hour arrived, I'm certain that the Great Room seemed like the Montauk Light House to the tiny beasts. I still chuckle when I think of the elegant Mrs. Timpson, in her Pucci gown, briskly pumping her old-fashioned FLIT gun at each wire-mesh screen in the Great Room.

My first duty after staff breakfast was to take Mr. Timpson's trousers and dinner jacket from his dressing room and 'refresh' them for the evening. I was the Butler/valet after all. The trousers were of very high quality and I pressed them in a flash. Conversely, his velour dinner jacket was a challenge. It was always creased and the creases couldn't be smoothed away.

But then I thought of a trick my friend Gordon Jones at Mar-a-Lago taught me. I took the dinner jacket to my quarters and turned on the hot water in my shower. Then I put the jacket on a wooden hanger and hung it on the shower rod and closed the door. Five minutes later, I entered a virtual steam room and took the jacket out. It seemed to have just returned from the dry cleaners. Mr. Timpson could never figure out just how I accomplished this feat so quickly.

Oddly enough, Mrs. Timpson enjoyed doing the house food-shopping herself. So, after discussing the menu for the coming few days with Molly, she drove her Cadillac six miles over the winding country roads to the Southampton A&P.

When her daughter, Hilles Hamersley Martin arrived with her children for a short stay, the house suddenly buzzed with activity. The subdued routine I had become accustomed to – ended abruptly along with my growing sense of boredom.

The blond, blue-eyed Martin children were exceptionally well mannered and called Mr. Timpson 'Uncle Bob.' They loved diving and swimming off the end of the pier and occasionally were joined by their grandmother. They also liked to boat and fish off the pier – but always with adult supervision, usually mine.

What delighted them most was flying their kites off the end of the pier. It was a perfect location because of the powerful updraft off the water. The children flew their kites with fishing poles whose reels provided the line for the kites. When they had finished they simply reeled in the kites like fish they caught in the sky. It was a scene worthy of Norman Rockwell.

When they dined with their grandparents the children were expected to conduct themselves in a manner in keeping with the formality of the lifestyle surrounding them. When the day's play was over, they bathed and changed into the appropriate attire. After they were seated at the table, they consumed their dinner slowly with perfect table manners and even joined the conversation. I was impressed.

I was free to do whatever I wanted every night after the diner service was over and the pantry was organized for the next morning's breakfast service.

My third requirement for accepting this position was to have a vehicle at my disposal after working hours. Since there were just two vehicles at the Marshlands – the Ford pick-up truck and Mrs. Timpson's Cadillac, the pick-up became my means of transportation.

About twenty minutes' drive through a succession of dark, meandering country roads was a popular dance-bar called 'The Millstone.' It was named for the antique, wheat-grinding millstone placed at its entrance. Surrounded by scrub-oak and pine trees amongst acres of potato fields, the Millstone' suddenly appeared like an oasis of light and sound. I went every night. On weeknights all sorts of vehicles squeezed into its small parking lot and the overflow parked, helter-skelter on both sides of the narrow country road. On weekends however, the Jaguars, BMWs and Mercedes arrived in droves. In that accumulation of luxury cars, my British-racing-green Ford pick-up with 'MARSHLANDS' emblazoned in gold leaf on both doors, stood out.

To a large degree Eastern Long Island is comprised of sand and so when leaving the 'The Millstone' patrons frequently discovered to their horror that their car had sunk into that soft sand and couldn't move.

And so the Marshlands pick-up came to their rescue. I pulled their cars out of the sand with its rear tow-hitch and chains. So, after my second or third rescue, not only were my drinks at the Millstone comped but I had earned a nickname which was – 'MARSHLANDS.'

"Here comes 'MARSHLANDS,' buy 'im a drink."

I occasionally stayed until the ungodly closing hour of three unless I found a willing partner for a bit of after-hours activity – I was after all, twenty-four years old – and always horny.

My last task was to inventory and pack the Timpson's Astor, Fish-Morris, Van Buren and Stuyvesant family sterling, along with the late Mr. Hammersley's yachting trophies into steamer trunks which would be kept in a Southampton bank vault in until the next Summer season.

Thinking ahead, I decided to contact Hildegarde Schine by phone. She told me her plans for the Winter season were still uncertain.

So I proposed traveling to Kloof Natal with the Timpsons as their Butler. I thought it would be an interesting adventure to see and experience South Africa. Mrs. Timpson told me that it was not possible. She didn't go into great detail as to her reason but assured me it wouldn't work. She was certain I would not be happy there.

Robert Clermont Livingston Timpson and is wife lived most of the year in Kloof (near Durban), KwaZulu Natal, South Africa where he was born and spent his early years. Under the apartheid government, domestic servants were mostly migrant workers from 'Bantustans,' the so-called homelands in South Africa for several different black ethnic groups. They all needed 'papers' to be allowed to work in white South Africa. If hired, they lived in all black 'townships' not far from their place of employment. At times female servants lived in quarters in or near the main house in order to insure their availability twenty-four hours a day. Their earnings were incredibly low and abuse, it was said – was routine.

Late one afternoon as I was packing up the last of the silver, Mrs. Timpson approached me in the Butler's pantry. She told me of how pleased she and her husband were with my performance and offered me the position of Butler/valet for the next Summer season with a raise in salary. I of course, accepted.

Shortly after the Timpsons left for London, I went back home. I enjoyed my interaction with Mrs. Timpson's perfect grandchildren so much that I decided to earn my college degree in: Early Childhood Education.

One morning as I was preparing to revisit the Madison Avenue agencies, my mother called me to the phone. It was Mrs. Schine. She told me she was feeling a lot better and having received very positive reports from her doctors, decided to reopen the house in Boca Raton for the Winter season. She asked if I was available. I said 'of course.' She suggested I start immediately at Four

East in New York and then go on to Boca. She added that there would be a handsome increase in salary.

Honestly, I loved working for Hildegarde Schine so it wasn't that difficult to accept. In any case, after what she attempted to do for me with Colonel Pixley, I would have worked the season for free.

So at last things were going my way. I was now set for the entire year before starting college. autumn, winter and spring in New York City and Boca Raton, summer in Southampton – and on to St. John's University in September. Nothing could have been more perfect.

Or so I thought.

Chapter Eight

Hildegarde Redux

A week later I was back at Four East where nothing had changed in two years. Mrs. Schine, now fully recovered from whatever ailed her, was as absorbed as ever in her countless charitable projects. Weather permitting, Mr. Schine continued to walk to and from his office in the Seagram Building. And C. Richard still lived in his cave-like bedroom, enjoying in his out-of-season fires. Addie and Hyacinth trucked on – and I drove the Rolls to my parents' house every night.

In early October Mrs. Schine decided that she, Mr. Schine, Addie and I would delight in the overwhelming splendor of Autumn at Myhil for two weeks. A week and a half later I drove the four of us up in Mr. Schine's limousine. Hyacinth would stay behind to care for C. Richard.

Since I had only seen Myhil from late spring until mid-August, I was not prepared for the spectacle that Mother Nature had in store. It was cool, clear and sunny with golden-yellow and scarlet-hued autumn leaves reflected in blue lakes. It seemed like Heaven on Earth.

One day Mrs. Schine told Addie and me that she decided to organize a dinner party for Mr. Schine's brother, his wife and another Gloversville couple. I was a bit bored and had lots of time on my hands so I decided to fashion an overly elaborate table-top display. So I carefully selected the suitable crystal, china, linens and silver for the event. To this I added seasonal fruits – apples, pears, grapes, pumpkins and an overabundance of the most colorful autumn leaves I could find. I created a table even Mrs. Post would have loved – it was simply glorious!

My enthusiasm for this undertaking also inspired Addie to new heights. From beginning to end the meal was one of the best she ever produced. The guests were overwhelmed for a number of reasons. The amalgam of the cuisine, the table settings and the service by someone (me) who knew the fine points of table etiquette occasioned a most wonderful evening. Both Schines were delighted.

When we returned to New York we began preparing for the annual trek to Boca. Addie and Hyacinth packed Mrs. Schine's clothes and I packed her favorite art objects. This time we didn't pile them into the Schines' cars. It seems that a Hertz Corporation board member was a relative of Mrs. Schine and had offered her a great 'deal' on the rental of large truck.

When Mrs. Schine learned of the truck's huge capacity she rose to the occasion. She decided to load the truck with numerous flats of canned food that she purchased at wholesale prices from the owner of Beatrice Foods – a close friend of the Schines.

She reasoned that the mass purchases would not only save a great deal of money on the food bill but also eliminate the need for daily grocery shopping in Boca.

The seemingly endless moving day began at six in the morning. First I drove the Rolls from my parents' house to the Schines' garage on East 66th Street. From there I taxied up to the Hertz location in the Bronx where I picked up the monster truck. Then I drove it to the nearby Beatrice Foods' warehouse where the flats of canned foods were loaded. From there I drove back to Four East where Mrs. Schine's clothes and art objects from the apartment were put on the truck and I finally made my way to the New Jersey Turnpike and began the drive south.

The truck was new and had automatic drive, a great radio and a very efficient heater. Once behind the wheel of this behemoth – vivid memories of my Army days flooded back. Although my rank was that of an N.C.O. acting Corporal, I was also required to drive an ambulance and a two and a half ton truck, dubbed a 'Duce and a half' on my unit's numerous maneuvers.

It had been a long and exhausting day and by the time I reached Camden, New Jersey night was falling and I decided to find a motel and get some sleep.

The next morning I skipped breakfast and hit the road shortly after sunrise. With a cup of coffee from the motel I continued my drive south. Interstate 95 was still not finished in Virginia and so I used the southbound Route 301. It snaked its way from one small town to another with an occasional stretch of completed I-95 in between.

Once in Virginia I decided to stop for breakfast and gas. I soon found the perfect location, a classic diner in built in conjunction with a Shell gas station. After breakfast, I climbed back into the truck and drove through the diner's parking lot to the gas station.

Typical of many Shell stations of the time, the structure over the pumps was gussied up to resemble a Swiss chalet. As I pulled into the station I heard a loud crunching sound immediately followed by an avalanche of debris and clouds of dust crashing down on the truck.

When the dust settled I realized I had just destroyed about a third of the Shell station's Swiss chalet roof by attempting to drive Mrs. Schine's gargantuan truck under it – OOPS!

The real concern of the people who ran over to see if I was hurt was reassuring. The gas station's owner and a local police officer soon arrived. Everyone was so calm, I began to wonder how often this sort of event occurred – as I recall there were no signs indicating 'Low Clearance Ahead.' I spent the rest of the morning dealing with this unforeseen, bizarre incident. I filled out the paperwork needed for the station's insurance company – and then I called Mrs. Schine.

True to form, her first concern was that I was all right and that no one else had been injured. Thank the Lord she had insisted on buying every kind of insurance Hertz offered.

When it was determined that no one else was involved, the remaining structure was shored up and the truck was carefully extricated. I was on my way again an hour later. Aside from minor dents and scratches the truck survived the disaster well – far better than the gas station's roof.

A day and a half later I arrived at the Schine compound in Boca Raton. All the Beatrice Foods canned goods – five flats worth – joined by Mrs. Schine's art works, bags of clothes and sundry items were carefully unloaded.

In the 1967 Winter season (my first year in the Army) Mrs. Shine decided that she would drive herself around Boca during the day. But it was a bit too much for her and by mid-Winter she found Freddie who became their full-time chauffeur and moved into my former suite. In the 1968 Winter season (my second year in the Army) that arrangement continued.

When I arrived for the 1969 Winter season, I met Freddie for the first time. Mrs. Schine hadn't mentioned him to me. Freddie was in his late thirties and of German or Austrian ancestry. He was blonde, six-feet tall and had an unfortunate lisp. I was obliged to share my quarters with him. Fortunately there *were* two bedrooms, but sadly for me – only *one* bathroom.

Freddie was a snob and a bore. He continually bragged about the fabulous families he had chauffeured in the past. His favorites were the 'Biddles.' I wanted to ask him, though I never did, "If the Biddles were so wonderful, why did you leave them?"

My major problem with Freddie was that he was gay and had decided that I was the man he was waiting for. He began speaking to me in unequivocal *double-entendres* in front of Addie and Hyacinth – and then he began to stalk me. He loitered behind every door. I showed no interest in him whatsoever – and he eventually gave up.

I never told Mrs. Schine who, in any event was oblivious to anyone's religion, race or sexual orientation.

The Schines' daily routine was frozen in time. Most evenings they dined alone at home. Occasionally they had an evening out – either attending a small dinner party at a friend's home or an event connected with some charitable function. I easily slipped back into my position as Mrs. Schine's Butler/man-Friday and made a conscious decision to never give Mr. Schine any reason to be unhappy with my dealings with his wife.

When I resumed doing Mrs. Schine's endless errands Freddie became Mr. Schine's personal driver. So every day after breakfast, Freddie drove him to his office three miles away. Since Mr. Schine rarely returned home for lunch, Freddie's sole responsibility for the rest of the day was to drive back to the office to pick him up and drive him back home. That made my life much easier since I had much less interaction with Mr. Schine.

He however adopted a strange late evening exercise routine. Sometime around nine or nine-thirty, he would leave the house and pace back and forth between the two entrance gates several times. Addie said that on his last round, usually sometime after ten, he would make sure the two sets of double gates were securely shut and latched from the inside. So therefore, after midnight when I returned from my outings, I was obliged to park the car outside on the road, climb over the latched gates, un-latch them, go back out and drive the car in. No one mentioned his bizarre behavior to Mrs. Schine. Addie, Hyacinth and I had grown quite adept at protecting Mrs. Schine from events that could upset her.

Many foreign species of animals and plants have invaded southern Florida. But one of the most offensive creatures that thrives there is a native – the raccoon. Walt Disney and his artists have bestowed this creature with charming and amusing characteristics. However, when one is confronted by a group of raccoons rummaging through bins of garbage for food scraps – a very different evaluation of the masked marauders emerges.

When the Schines' house was built in the 1950s, the latest trend was to have kitchen garbage bins countersunk into the ground outside the back door. When a foot-pedal was pressed, the lid snapped open to receive its allotment of trash and when released it fell back and slammed closed with a loud noise.

A family of raccoons had made it part of their daily routine to rummage for food scraps in the garbage bins and leave a disgusting mess behind as proof of their visit.

Addie, Hyacinth and I made many attempts to dissuade them of their habit. The first was pouring ammonia both into and around the bins. We hoped the noxious fumes would drive them away – they didn't. We tried separating the moist food scraps from the dry garbage and putting them into a more secure bin – no luck. In utter frustration we tried placing bricks on every lid – they were pushed off. Finally we put a ten-pound cinder block on top of each lid – that failed as well.

One February evening after the Schines had gone up to their quarters and we had reached the end of our workday, Addie was finishing up in the kitchen when a loud noise came from outside the back door. We realized that it was the raccoons foraging for scraps in the bins.

Addie had devised a new battle plan to dissuade the raccoon family. She took down several large metal pots and began to fill them with a combination of several squirts of dishwashing soap and ammonia. She finished her concoction by adding *extremely* hot tap water.

Addie was determined to teach those nasty little critters a lesson. She called on Hyacinth and me to assist her. So the three of us left the kitchen with pots of hot, soapy ammonia water in hand and headed outside to where the garbage bins were under siege. We were a force to be reckoned with!

Addie turned on the outside floodlights and we saw standing before us – five adult raccoons clutching food scraps in their ugly little claws. They froze in place.

Addie was the first to attack with the largest pot. Our plan was that after Addie delivered the first volley, I would follow with the second. Then to finish this attack Hyacinth would deliver the *coup-de-grâce* with hers. That would surely teach them a lesson they'd never forget!

The raccoon family was neither frightened nor defeated by Addie's volley. As soon as the initial shock wore off – the gang of five united, and standing upright on their hind paws, began lumbering towards us *'en masse'* all the while hissing in a most alarming manner.

Addie shouted, "Throw the god-damn pots at them!" but both Hyacinth and I decided this had been a terrible plan of attack and, throwing our liquid-laden pots in the air, made a mad dash back to the kitchen. Addie followed – I had never realized that Hyacinth and Addie could move so quickly. Their piercing screams sounded like a Marx Brothers comedy.

Seconds later we were safely inside the solidly-bolted kitchen door. Believe it or not those little buggers attacked the door and left their marks of indignation for all to see. The next day Mrs. Schine called a professional pest control agency and we never saw those horrid creatures again. Live and learn.

In mid-February a rare cold front descended on Boca with a vengeance. The thermometer plunged to the mid 40s. The Schines' house, as did most others in the sub-tropical town, had rooms with vaulted ceilings and glass walls – some doubling as sliding glass doors that led to their patios and pools. It was impossible to adequately heat those rooms in those unusually low temperatures.

Moreover, the bedrooms, guest rooms, staff quarters and other secondary rooms were also bitter-cold despite the fact that they had electric baseboard heaters.

But Mrs. Schine had an idea.

In 1970 there was a large Sears on US 1 just south of Boca Raton. In addition, there were several small appliance stores nearby. Her idea was to send me out to purchase as many space heaters as I could find. If the local vendors ran out, I was told to head south to Boynton Beach and Fort Lauderdale in search of more. I was instructed not to return until I bought eight heaters for the bedrooms, three for the living room, three for her office and two for the dining room. I drove off in the station-wagon with several credit cards and high hopes. I bought the first ten in Boca Raton and the remaining six in Boynton Beach.

When I returned I found Mrs. Schine in her office wrapped head-to-toe in her furs. She was delighted to see me and the large number of heaters I bought. I unpacked them and set them up in their designated locations.

Mid-way through my task I had a feeling that something was amiss. I realized that I had not seen Addie or Hyacinth. I couldn't imagine where they were and I began to worry.

I glanced out of one of the sliding glass doors that led to the pool and saw a red light glowing in a very unlikely place – the entrance to the sauna. I ran out, pulled open the door and there they were – seated in the hot sauna, fully dressed. How brilliant!

Three days later the winter blast ended.

In addition to his previously-discussed situation, Freddie had no idea of how to properly maintain an automobile – the traditional bailiwick of a chauffeur. Details like – checking the tire pressure, the level of the distilled water in the battery, the window-washing compound and, most importantly – the engine oil, were overlooked. Mr. Schine's Cadillac limousine *was* four years old and had a lot of mileage, but had been well-maintained. However, Freddie did nothing except fill its tank when necessary and keep it clean.

The preparation for the move back to New York was proceeding well. All that remained to accomplish was the last-minute packing of our personal items.

As usual, Mr. and Mrs. Schine intended to fly back to New York. Addie was getting on in years and so Mrs. Schine, with her usual consideration and kindness, decided to fly both Addie and Hyacinth up as well.

I was to drive the Rolls up and Freddie, Mr. Schine's Cadillac limousine. The winters I was away, Addie and Hyacinth drove the Cadillac and Freddie the Rolls. Freddie was given a plane ticket back to West Palm Beach where he spent the summer months with his mother. As usual, the other cars would be driven to Myhil by local drivers.

The day before our drive commenced, I had a late lunch at poolside. At about three-thirty I heard a loud commotion from inside the house. Mr. Schine had returned from his office early and was furious.

It seems that on the ten-minute drive from Mr. Schine's office to the house – a serious problem with the car occurred. As Freddie drove over the new Intracoastal bridge the engine froze due to the lack transmission oil and the car simply died. Mr. Schine fired Freddie on the spot and flagged down a passing driver who graciously drove him home.

Upon arriving, he phoned his garage and told them to tow the car off the bridge and take Freddie into town – but not to the house.

An hour or so after Mr. Schine's return a taxi arrived at the house and Freddie got out and went directly to his room. By that time, Addie, Hyacinth, Mrs. Schine, and I were all well aware of the full story. Freddie never showed up for dinner. He was packing since he had been ordered to leave the premises before noon the next day.

The Cadillac limousine was towed to the local dealership for evaluation. They determined that the engine had been destroyed and had to be replaced. Taking into consideration its vintage and mileage, Mr. Schine decided to scrap it.

Before I began working for the Schines and while I was away in the Army the Schines had hired a professional to drive the Rolls down to Boca for the Winter season and back up to New York at its end. Addie always drove Mr. Schine's limousine both ways.

Since all the other vehicles were being driven to Myhil for the summer, the station-wagon, which was ordinarily left behind would have to substitute for Mr. Schine's defunct limousine. Mr. Schine contacted the professional driver who was available but he wanted to drive the Rolls – so I drove the station-wagon.

We arrived at Four East in the early afternoon. With the help of three of the building's obliging employees both vehicles were expeditiously unloaded. Then the driver and I drove both of them to the East Sixty-seventh Street garage. All I had left to do was to bid good-bye to Mrs. Schine.

She wished me luck in college and gave me an unexpectedly generous bonus.

(Addendum: J. Myer Schine kept all his Gloversville properties and some Florida real estate for a time. He died in 1971 at the age of eighty-one. At the time of his death it was determined that suffered from an undetected brain tumor.)

Chapter Nine

Hilles Timpson Redux

Mayhem

I arrived back in New York in early May and once again moved into my parents' home where I relaxed for a few weeks. With pleasant memories of my first phase of employment with the Timpsons, I was looking forward to a second, longer one, as their full Butler/valet since Mr. Roland had been promoted to Steward.

Mr. Roland picked me up at the Southampton station. When we entered the Marshlands he made a detour to show me the recently completed, year-round 'cottage' which the Timpsons had built for him – the new Steward and his wife. It was a large and attractive house set back several hundred yards from the main house. I confess I was taken aback by the generosity the Timpsons had shown in doing this.

It seems that Mr. Roland made an agreement with them to be the year-round caretaker of the property, i.e., the Steward – on the condition that a separate residence would be provided for him and his wife. The new structure more than filled the bill.

In the main house Molly, the cook welcomed me back in the staff dining room. She too had returned for a second season and would be assisted by Anna, a young kitchen aid. There was also an agreeable new parlor-maid/waitress Janet, who was quite accomplished at waiting table.

The Timpsons quickly settled into their relaxed, vacation schedule. And I had use of the Marshlands pick-up once again and spent many happy evenings dancing at the Millstone until the wee hours. The guests, all family, were few but always delightful. Even the tiny flying 'beasts' the blight of the Great Room were under control that summer.

Nine weeks flew by quickly and easily. I was beginning to daydream about my upcoming, belated entrance into college.

Tuesday was Molly's day off but she volunteered to make staff lunch before leaving for her hair-salon appointment later that afternoon. We had all been informed that the Timpsons would not lunch at home that day and so wouldn't require the staff's attention until the evening cocktail ritual began. Molly arranged that her capable assistant, Anna would prepare both the staff's and the Timpson's dinner that night. Consequently, my day would be stress-free – or so I thought!

Just after staff lunch Molly asked for a favor. It seemed she had found a new hairdresser she liked, but his salon was in Riverhead – the service-town twenty miles west of Southampton. To get there she told me she would have to take a taxi to Southampton and then a bus to Riverhead. She queried if I might consider giving her a ride to Riverhead.

Molly knew that I had permission to use the Marshland truck anytime I wanted and since I was free that day, I agreed. Molly said after he finished work for the day, her hairdresser would drive her back to the Marshlands.

Janet, the parlor-maid agreed to be 'on call' for phone calls or unexpected deliveries. So at twelve fifteen Molly and I were off to Riverhead.

It was a wonderful summer day without a cloud in the sky. The salty scent of the nearby ocean lay heavily on the air. The drive to and back from Riverhead would take less than an hour. Much to Molly's delight we were several minutes early. Having finished my good deed, I drove slowly back to the Marshlands on the more picturesque back roads.

As I neared the two ancient trees guarding the estate entrance, I down-shifted the pick-up from third to second gear in order to use its momentum to carry me up and over the slight incline in the road. But …

I couldn't believe what I saw! The sea anchor chain that always lay on the ground was now suspended between the two giant trees and was blocking the entrance. I hit the brakes hard. They screeched and the pick-up skidded and swerved and came to a rest inches from one of the trees. I caught my breath, put the pick-up in neutral, turned off the engine and jumped out to evaluate the situation.

With my heart pounding, I inspected the ponderous chain. I was astonished to see that it had been lifted from the ground and hooked on to the opposite tree which raised it to the level of the pick-up's headlights – a feat that required a great physical exertion. I unhooked it and drove back to the house. I was upset and thought, "What kind of practical joker would have done this idiotic thing?" Perhaps juvenile pranksters had perpetrated this villainous deed. It would have wrecked the front end of the pick-up – and I could have been hurt – or even killed.

When I entered the house Anna and Janet were seated at the staff dining table. I shouted,

"Who the hell put up that god-damned chain at the entrance?"

They looked at each other with glances of discomfort – they obviously knew something. So again, I asked,

"Who did it?"

Young Janet, never having seen this side of me, timidly answered,

"It was Mr. Timpson."

"Why in God's name did he do such a stupid thing?" I demanded to know.

Slowly she replied,

"Just after you and Molly left, Mr. Timpson came into the kitchen and said, "Tell Thomas I changed my plans and want my lunch to be served on the deck in half an hour."

When we told him that you drove Molly to Riverhead for her hair appointment, he went crazy. He said he was going to teach you a lesson and lock you off the property. Janet, glancing up at Anna for approval, said,

"We didn't think he'd put up the chain."

Anna added, "I volunteered to prepare his lunch and Janet could certainly have served it. But he said *NO*, he only wanted you."

I concluded that the reason for Mr. Timpson's tantrum was clear – he simply forgot he was not in South Africa. What was I thinking when I asked to go there as their Butler last year?

The gulf between the Timpsons' South African servants and their staff in Southampton was vast and unbridgeable. But while I believed the Timpsons treated their servants better than most others in Kloof, I also understood it certainly had to initiate a 'mindset change' each summer for them to re-adjust to the American way of dealing with employees.

In a way I was re-living my confrontation with Mr. Schine. But while he had merely thrown food at me, Mr. Timpson put my life at risk. What to do? I decided that I would wait until Mrs. Timpson returned later that afternoon and tell her what happened.

When she came home at about four-thirty we met in the Butler's pantry. I related the bizarre event that had transpired. Needless to say she was quite upset. She could hardly believe that her husband had had such an unreasonable reaction to something that was quite honestly – his own doing.

I told her how fortunate it was that I was the first to come upon the chain since when she was returning from her shopping trips she always approached the entrance from the east and, just as I had done, accelerated a little to glide over the rise onto the private road. From that vantage point, she would not have noticed the chain until it was too late. Very few people used seat belts those days so had she collided with the chain she would have gone right through the windshield. I told her that I thought her husband owed both of us an apology.

After a few moments of silence passed, her reply was not what I expected. She simply stated that her husband would never admit that he was misguided in any of his actions.

So I told her that under the circumstances, even though I loved working at the Marshlands, I would leave the next morning. She said she understood.

And that evening, in my best 'Livingston' fashion, I performed the dinner service flawlessly. The Timpsons, usually quite garrulous, dined in utter silence and for the very first time, skipped their after dinner coffee in the Great Room and retired.

The next morning I packed my belongings and had my final breakfast at the Marshlands. Molly was upset and blamed herself for everything. She handed me an envelope with my check and a carefully phrased Reference that Mrs. Timpson had written. I accepted it, kissed her cheek and told her how lovely her hair looked.

A few weeks later in the fall of 1970 I began my four-year college stint at St. John's University. To earn some money during the summer breaks, I once again searched out temporary buttling jobs. Two stand out.

Chapter Ten

The Frick and I

The Kid Brother I Never Had

My first year of college was draining. It appeared I was the oldest freshman at St. John's, an oddity that precluded me from making many friends. In many cases, I was the same age or older than some of my instructors.

For my first summer break from college I decided to relax at home and not work. Instead I took summer courses at St. John's before the second year began. However, a year later when my second summer break arrived, my savings had diminished and I needed to find a job.

Since no temporary job would pay as much as Buttling would, I went back to the Hedland in early June. They told me that one Mr. I. Townsend Burden II in Locust Valley, Long Island was looking for a temporary Butler. That sounded perfect. So I borrowed my father's car and drove to his Long Island mansion for my interview.

I arrived at an English Tutor-style structure that reminded me of Fairholme in Newport. The house itself was a nineteenth-century, English Tudor-style confection. It was reputably built for a family member – a niece of J. P. Morgan.

I rang the front doorbell and Liz Johnson, the Housekeeper/cook greeted me at the door. She led me to the reception room where two people were chatting on a sofa. They were Mr. Burden, a recent widower and his Social Secretary, Annie Redmond.

Mr. Burden received me warmly, told me to sit and asked to see my References – a standard request. They both read them and Mr. Burden said, "Quite impressive young man – is that all of them?"

I clutched. I was aware that a so-called 'grapevine' existed between potential employers and their higher staff and I thought that he had possibly heard of my problem with Mrs. Young – so I decided to restate it from my point of view.

I relaxed and told them the story. It seemed that Mrs. Young had attained a legendary status with the Social Register crowd in respect to her severe and demanding requirements. They both laughed heartily – and I was hired.

Mrs. Redmond later told me that it was my dramatic and hilarious rendition of Mrs. Young and the missing dinner bell clapper that landed me the job.

I was hired as Butler but they really had no need of a Butler in that easy household. My sole responsibility would be to look after Mr. Burden's youngest child, Dixon Frick Burden who was nearing seventeen. My job was to be his companion and his 'wheels' – since he was too young to drive. Mr. Burden handed me the keys to his late wife's automobile – a four-door, British-racing-green Cadillac Fleetwood, which I would use to chauffeur young Frick. I drove home happily in my father's car and the next morning my father drove me back to the Burden house.

Frick lost his mother the year before and was at 'sixes and sevens.' But it seemed to me that he was simply in need of someone to 'hang out' with. We hit it off from the start and we became lifelong friends.

The long entrance hall was the heart of the house. It ran the entire length of the building – from the front door to the great lawn and pool beyond. From it, double doors led to a formal dining room, a library and a sun-filled living room. A grand staircase on its left side led to the second floor bedroom suites. At the far end of the hall – a long gallery led to an unused grand ballroom.

All the front rooms were furnished with superb English and American antiques. Most memorable to me were the numerous paintings, handed down from previous generations. Like Fairholme, the front and back of the house were connected by several doors.

In its heyday the house had a sizeable staff. It had a large kitchen, a Butler's pantry and a staff dining room on the ground floor of the back of the house. Once a well-stocked wine cellar occupied the cool basement – but in 1972 it was filled with old steamer trunks, broken bicycles and unused furniture.

The two-story staff wing was accessed by stairs off the kitchen. But when I arrived it was virtually vacant. Only Eva May, the parlor-maid/waitress lived there. Liz Johnson lived in her own home in nearby Westbury. I was assigned the rather large, Butler's quarters.

In the summer of 1972 Mr. Burden was a recent widower. His deceased wife and the mother of his children was Frances Frick. She was the daughter of paleontologist Childs Frick – the son of the industrialist and art collector, Henry Clay Frick.

Their union produced five children – Frances, their eldest child and only daughter was nicknamed 'Dixie' and her four brothers – I. Townsend III, called 'Townie,' Henry, Childs and my charge, their youngest child, 'Frick.'

Frick's three brothers were not in the house that summer. His eldest brother, Townie was married and lived in Washington, D.C. Henry and Childs were on summer break from college and traveling.

His sister Dixie had come home during the last stages of her mother's illness and was spending much of her time in the Hamptons with friends. So, that summer of 1972, the sole inhabitants of the cavernous mansion were – Eva May, six King Charles Spaniels, a black cat named Sputie – Frick, and me.

Mr. Burden spent most of his time in New York City with his friends at their private clubs. From time to time, he returned to Locust Valley for a few days. When he came home he dined alone in his den from a tray. So there was really no Buttling for me to do.

As the summer passed Mr. Burden was invited to an ever-increasing number of dinner parties at his friends' homes. He was after all a wealthy, good looking man in his late fifties – *and* a year had passed since his wife's passing.

Since society hostesses, relentless matchmakers all, were always on the lookout for eligible bachelors and widowers, Mr. Burden became the 'man of the hour.'

Frick and I usually had our meals in the kitchen or on snack trays that we took to the library to watch something or other on TV.

The Burden household was, to use a 1970's term, 'laid-back.' *All* my other employers (except for Mrs. Schine – a liberal thinker and friend to all,) had white staff – with no exceptions. But not here! – both Liz and Eva May were of African-American descent.

Eva May was a slender woman with a radiant smile and was of an indeterminable age. She laughed a lot and wore gold-rimmed glasses. Her job description was 'parlor-maid/waitress' but in reality, she did everything but cook. In any case, the house itself required little attention. The formal rooms on the first floor and the numerous bedrooms and baths on the second were hardly used. Liz, who had been with the family for years, was the Housekeeper/cook. Both she and Eva-May were among the most pleasant, warm and competent individuals I'd ever worked with.

Liz arrived early every morning and prepared breakfast for the three of us. Frick didn't often make an appearance at that early hour.

The King Charles Spaniels were the remaining members of our 'family.' The breed is admired for its silky coat with 'feathered' ears and paws. All six were beauties – albeit high-strung and high-spirited. Liz called them the 'gang.'

The 'gang' had the run of the house and grounds in all kinds of weather. They had access and egress through a two-way 'doggie-door' in the entrance hall. The estate was extremely large and, in addition to the beautifully-landscaped formal areas surrounding the house, had acres of native woodland.

When Liz called the 'gang' into the house at feeding time it was always a mad scramble, especially on rainy days. Picture the six of them – soaking wet, barking madly, knots and twigs in their coats, with their twenty-four mud-soaked paws sliding over the wood floors.

In the long gallery that led to the unused grand ballroom was a large settee, which was doubtlessly passed down from an illustrious ancestor. It was referred to as the 'The Dog's Bed.' At any time of the day when there was nothing else to interest them, the 'gang' could be found heaped together and sleeping soundly on that lovely piece of furniture.

In the summer of 1973 Mr. Burden, to the chagrin of the society matchmakers, married Annie Redmond. The newlyweds decided to sell the mansion and move to an American Colonial house on nearby Feeks Lane. The Dog's Bed as well as several other pieces of furniture were appraised for the move.

The Dog's Bed was discovered to be an American antique of significant value. I believe it was given to Frick's sister Dixie, who was living in Bryn Mawr, Pennsylvania with her husband.

The Burdens kept a nineteen-foot Boston Whaler power-boat moored at the Seawanhaka Yacht Club on Centre Island in Oyster Bay. Frick and I spent many a sun-drenched afternoon boating on Long Island Sound. The days flew by – blending one into another. Frick, my junior by some eight years became the little brother I never had. We spent our evenings with the six dogs and listened to music, watched old movies on TV and ate the homemade 'munchies' Liz left in the pantry fridge.

Frick had an attractive girlfriend named Meg and together they imagined their own 'dream date.' They wanted to see *Godspell,* a popular off-Broadway show, and afterwards go to dinner and then disco dancing. I would accompany them as both their chaperone and driver. After they both received their parents' permission, Annie Redmond bought us three great theater seats.

I, of course, was designated the person in charge of the adventure. I suggested dining at Hippopotamus, New York's 'in spot,' that was owned by Richard Burton's ex-wife Sybil Burton. After dinner we would go downstairs and join the disco dancing for an hour or so.

Foolishly we had overlooked our post-theater expenses – like the bill for dinner. It was only after the bill arrived that Frick and I became acutely aware of our rather embarrassing financial situation and neither one of us had a credit card.

Annie Redmond had given me three hundred dollars but I had already spent thirty for the garage near the theater and allotted another thirty for the garage near the Hippopotamus. Frick had thirty dollars so together we had enough to pay the restaurant bill, but not a fair gratuity. We decided that Meg should leave and wait in the lobby and we would remain at the table. When she was out of sight, we paid the bill and left. I'm sure the tip we left was the smallest one our waiter ever received. We put the disco off for another time and drove home.

The house was empty in August. So I asked Liz if she thought it was possible to have some friends and my parents over for a barbeque party at the pool. She thought for a moment and, in her usual understated manner, smiled and said,

"I'll look into it!"

The next day Liz informed me that since my guest list included my parents there was no problem. It was understood that, with the exception of the use of the guest bathroom in the front hall, the interior of the house was – Off Limits. And so the phone invitations went out.

It was a perfect day. By noon the party was well underway. Somehow my 'small' gathering had grown a bit larger than originally planned. At least eighteen people arrived. Thank goodness my parents were there.

About my parents – my mother was a Saint. On the other hand my father was a New York City Cop, shortly to retire with the rank of Detective, First Class. Be assured, in their presence nothing improper would have had the slightest chance of happening. However, strange things *can* happen when least expected.

The pool party was well under way when the need to replenish ice arose. I asked my father to help me and we went inside. I asked him to simply wait for me in the entrance hall since I could dash into the kitchen and return quickly with the next two bags of ice.

When I returned I found my father exceptionally subdued. Not giving this a second thought, we returned to the party. Everyone was having a wonderful time. All was well!

Only days later did I become aware of the events that took place in my very short absence. It seems that in the few minutes I left my father alone in the front hall, Dixie Burden, Frick's sister appeared in the house to get a few items she had forgotten to pack. She had been scheduled to be in the Hamptons for the entire weekend.

My father, ever the dutiful Cop, confronted the 'stranger' entering the house and demanded to know,

"Who are *You?* and what's *Your Name?*"

Truly down to earth Dixie, simply replied, "I'm Dixie Burden, I live here. Who are you?" To which my father, realizing his faux-pas, sheepishly replied,

"Oh, I'm sorry. I'm Tom's father."

As it turned out, Dixie had not been informed by either Liz, Annie Redmond or Mr. Burden, that I had permission to have the pool party.

I learned these facts several days later when Dixie, having returned from the Hamptons, said over morning her coffee that she had 'accidently' met my father in the front hall at my party.

Several days later, in a phone conversation with my mother, I inquired if she was aware of my father's brief meeting with Dixie. Her reply was that Dad had mentioned in passing that he met the young lady of the house and found her most charming.

The rest of the summer passed quickly and before I knew it I was back at college. One mid-winter day Annie Redmond phoned me at home. She said she was planning a dinner party at the Burden house and asked if I would be available to put my Buttling skills to work. I accepted. I was on Christmas break and a little extra cash at that time of year was always welcome.

Numerous Buttling opportunities for Mr. Burden and his friends followed. Thanks to Annie Redmond these lucrative jobs continued through the late winter and early spring.

Sometime in late May I received a call from Mrs. Redmond who asked if I had made plans for the upcoming summer. Frick had come of age and no longer needed me to be his 'wheels.' I told her that at the moment I had no plans. She told me that she had a job for my consideration. It seemed that her friend Pamela Tower LeBoutillier's mother needed a Butler for the summer. She asked if I was interested in the job.

"Absolutely!" I said.

Mrs. LeBoutillier's mother was none other than Mrs. George Macculloch Miller née Flora Vanderbilt Whitney, the daughter of Gertrude Vanderbilt Whitney (the sculptress of note and the founder of the Whitney Museum of American Art) and a first cousin of Jock Hay Whitney.

An added benefit was that there was no agency fee for accepting the position. Perfect!

(Addendum: Sadly my friend Dixon Frick Burden died on the nineteenth of December 2013 in a freak accident in Colorado.)

Chapter Eleven

Flora Vanderbilt Whitney Miller

Her Mother's Daughter

In early June Annie Redmond's friend Pamela (Mrs. Thomas LeBoutillier) interviewed me for the position of Butler in the Old Westbury 'Country Home' of her widowed, seventy-six year old mother, Mrs. George Macculloch Miller. I knew the area well and was looking forward to the interview.

These 'Country Homes' were much more than summer retreats. The American super-rich were divided into two groups – the 'horsey-set' who played Polo and the 'yacht racing-set' who raced ocean-going yachts.

The horsey-set found flat Old Westbury, Long Island the ideal location for breeding horses and playing Polo. The 'yacht racing-set' found Newport, Rhode Island on the ocean, their ideal choice.

I arrived early for the interview and parked my father's car on the drive, then walked to the front door (since I refused to use the 'Service' entrance) and rang the door-bell. The door opened and there stood Margaret, Mrs. Miller's personal maid. My first impression was that she had an air of superiority and viewed me as some sort of interloper. She must have realized that I would be hired with or without her approval, so she led me through the entry hall into the grand living room.

Seated at the far end of the room were Mrs. Miller and her daughter Pamela, sipping tea. They both smiled and asked me to sit and offered me a cup of tea which I graciously accepted. The interview itself was like a classic afternoon tea party.

The usual questions were asked. However, with my glowing References from Frank Moffat at Mar-a-Lago, Hildegarde Schine, Hilles Timpson and Annie Redmond of course, the outcome was never in question.

I did however present my usual conditions. I required that my quarters come with a private bath and I asked to use the estate wagon in the evenings and on my day off.

Pamela LeBoutillier and her mother had been prepped by Annie Redmond and my demands were met. I was now to be the summer Butler for a member of one of America's most prominent families.

The house was a fifteen thousand square foot Georgian-style mansion surrounded by formal gardens. It was built in 1926 and had been occupied by Flora Miller since 1942. It was filled with the accumulated art collection of her Whitney and Vanderbilt forbearers.

Off the living room was an enclosed porch which had, in lieu of solid walls, floor-to-ceiling mesh screens that caught each fragrant zephyr on those sultry summer days. Flora Miller spent long afternoons there surrounded by beautiful *objets d'art*, tropical plants and flowers, relaxing and reading in her mother's red-lacquered, Chinese 'opium' bed. She was still a beautiful woman – virtually wrinkle-free, always well-coiffed and perfectly made up

She was deeply involved with the Whitney Museum – first as a trustee, then as the vice president, then president and chairman and beginning in 1974 as honorary chairman – a position she held until her death in 1986. She married twice and had two children from each union.

In 1923 Flora's parents, Gertrude Vanderbilt and Harry Payne Whitney began constructing a Norman-style house called 'French House' on Whitney land near their home in Old Westbury.

It was planned as a summer home for Flora and her husband Roderick Tower and their two small children (Pamela and her brother, Whitney.) However, before the house was finished – the couple divorced.

Flora spent the summer of 1925 with her children at her mother's studio in Paris. Later that year she met her second husband, George Macculloch Miller, a principal in the architectural firm of Noel & Miller.

Smitten, he followed Flora to Egypt where she and her children had joined her mother. Gertrude was in Egypt finding inspiration in the ancient monuments for a sculptural commission she had received.

In 1927 Flora and George married in Cairo. They lived in New York City and summered in 'French House.' Flora had two children with George – a daughter, Flora and a son, Leverett.

When Gertrude Vanderbilt Whitney died in 1942, Flora and George Miller left French House and moved into her nearby mansion.

French House and its thirty-six surrounding acres became part of the New York Institute of Technology in 1963. I saw it for the first time when I arrived for work in June of 1973. It looked abandoned and was in dreadful condition. The property was sold in 1999 and the house was torn down a year later.

Flora Miller lived alone. Her live-in staff consisted of seven people – Mildred, the cook and her kitchen aid; John, the chauffeur and his wife Margaret who was Flora Miller's personal maid, Ana, the parlor-maid/waitress, was French and an artist in her own right. Tommy the houseman and I were hired just for that summer. Frank, the gardener and his wife, the laundress were day help who went home each night. Ana was permitted to live and work in the former studio of Flora's mother Gertrude Vanderbilt Whitney. The studio, designed by the firm of Delano and Aldrich in 1913, still stands.

Margaret's cold reception on the day of my interview should have sounded an alarm. With the exception of Ana and Tommy, a young man who was the temporary summer employee for heavy work, all the rest were the usual – middle-aged 'professional lackeys.'

Like Mrs. Young's crew at Fairholme, many had come from families that had been 'in service' for generations. From the get-go they were suspicious of me and avoided contact with me – the *temporary* 'college-boy' Butler.

Despite my experience with their mind-set before, I still found their attitude strange when, taking into consideration that they knew I was engaged only for the summer and furthermore, I was hired through the Burdens – personal friends of Mrs. Miller's daughter – one would think it would make for a somewhat greater acceptance but it didn't – and it just got worse.

As Butler I was the top of the household pecking order. While the Butler's principal duty consists of the supervision and serving of the luncheon and dinner services, an important part of his responsibility is to keep the Butler's pantry well provisioned and to order the essential items from the local estate purveyors.

At that time Westbury was the so-called 'service-town' for the large estates in the vicinity. My sojourn with the Burdens the summer before had apprised me of the best purveyors of food and supplies in Westbury. So while I was at it I inventoried the cook's larder and the storeroom of household cleaning and laundry supplies. Then I placed the order that would cover the needs of the household for at least two weeks.

However, unbeknownst to me, Mrs. Miller's cook Mildred preferred to order even the basic non-perishable (canned) food every two or three days. And Margaret, in addition to being Flora Miller's personal lady's maid, regarded herself as the Housekeeper. If so, she should have known that she was in charge of ordering all the non-food related items. I quickly realized that Margaret and Mildred were both ignorant of their duties and utterly inefficient.

Both of them threw a fit. They ganged up on me in the kitchen and blatantly accused me of 'making a deal' for a 'kickback' from the purveyors which of course, wasn't true.

I could only guess that I had unintentionally deprived them of a source of income that they regarded as their rightful fringe benefit. No wonder they were angry. I knew that this kickback routine was a tradition with old-school domestics who were after all, famously underpaid.

So I told them that when the supplies I had ordered ran out they could resume requisitioning them in their preferred way. I decided not to enlighten Mrs. Miller with the fact that her trusted 'old-retainers' were padding the bills. It might have upset her. But, then again Mrs. Miller having been 'to-the-manor-born,' more likely than not, would have considered it 'just the way things are done.'

One afternoon her son Leverett arrived to have lunch with his mother. During lunch I heard him ask Mrs. Miller if it was possible to borrow the estate wagon for two weeks or so. He needed it because he was going on a camping trip with his son in upstate New York. Mrs. Miller replied that because of the agreement she'd made with me – she couldn't.

After lunch Leverett, as unaffected as his mother, found me in the pantry and asked if I had a moment to discuss something? A bit confused I said, "Of course."

Then he asked an unusual question,

"Tom, would you consider exchanging my Aston-Martin for the estate wagon for two or three weeks?"

Boy, tough decision! – a British sports car for the station-wagon – "Yes," I answered.

John, the chauffeur was having lunch in the next room and he overheard the exchange. If only I had had a camera to capture the expressions that swept across his face – disbelief – anger – rage – all directed at me.

As it happened, I drove Leverett's extraordinary vehicle for close to three weeks. When I worked at the Burdens I made several friends my own age in the nearby towns of Muttontown,

Oyster Bay, and Old Brookville so I visited them frequently. I didn't venture far from the estate. Only once did I go into the city for a friend's birthday party. I was so anxious about leaving the car on the street that I parked it in an Upper East Side garage. Aside from a champagne toast for the birthday boy, I drank only ginger ale – the safety of Leverett's car was my top priority.

In 1973 the nation was captivated by thirty-seven days of live television coverage of the Watergate hearings in Washington. Mrs. Miller was no exception. She watched the hearings daily on a television set in a corner of her living room. One afternoon I brought her an iced tea. She asked me to sit down and watch the hearings with her and I did. I watched them with Mrs. Miller several times after that.

My afternoon 'Watergate tea' with Mrs. Miller was anathema to her old-school staff. They began debating my unspeakable transgression in front of me at the staff dining table so I began to take my meals alone in the Butler's pantry. Even so, their comments were so loud, I could hear them (which of course was their intension.)

The *coup-de-grâce* to my relationship with the staff took place with the arrival of my invitation to the wedding of Mr. Burden to Annie Redmond. My invitation arrived the very same time as Mrs. Miller's. Each was in an identical Tiffany & Co. hand-calligraphed envelope and it didn't take Margaret too long to find out what was inside.

They couldn't deal with the fact that their world was changing. For them, the idea that I, a staff member, would receive an identical engraved invitation to the wedding of their employer's good friends as she did, was just too much. They never spoke directly to me again. I loved that!

Mrs. Miller dined alone most evenings. She did stage a few small luncheons for friends and relatives that summer but in August she threw a fabulous dinner party. The occasion was her first cousin John 'Jock' Whitney's sixty-ninth birthday.

At the time 'Jock' Whitney was one of the ten richest men in the world. He was Ambassador to the Court of St. James under President Eisenhower, he was publisher of the New York Herald Tribune, he was a champion polo player (in March, 1933 the twenty-eight year old 'Jock' was on the cover of Time Magazine.) He was a generous philanthropist, a collector of fine American and French paintings *and* – a ladies' man of distinction.

Twelve guests attended. The dinner, mostly family, went off without a hitch and everyone was delighted. The guest of honor was extremely gracious. I later learned his name didn't appear in the Social Register since he had denounced that publication as 'undemocratic.'

Leverett's sister, Flora Miller Biddle decided to write a biography of her grandfather Harry Payne Whitney. So that summer she arrived at her grandmother's house (where her mother was living) to rummage through the vast accumulation of family papers and correspondence that was stored in the attic.

In the course of her search she discarded numerous, mostly hand-written notes that she deemed irrelevant. Scores of overflowing wastebaskets went through the Butler's pantry daily and I read some of them.

The notes provided a fascinating glimpse into the routines of the very rich in the early days of the twentieth century. There were countless 'Thank-You' notes from guests who had attended functions at Gertrude Vanderbilt Whitney's 'Country Home.'

The quality of the paper (with the watermark of Tiffany & Co. or Cartier) was extraordinary. And the beauty of the penmanship would bring tears to the eyes of any calligrapher today.

There were also weekly schedules listing the time weekend guests were to be 'collected' at the train station, their room assignments and special needs – such as their favorite flowers and teas and the foods they would or would not eat.

Sadly, they all made their way to the dustbin. I should have saved them.

When summer's end arrived, I left Mrs. Miller's employ almost reluctantly – she was a kind and beautiful woman and truly easy to work for. But my final year of college was just days away.

Pamela LeBoutillier wrote a charming Reference for me. And in my last year of college, Annie Redmond Burden arranged for me to work several private cocktail and dinner parties in both New York City and Long Island.

Chapter Twelve

Alva Bernheimer Gimbel

Married to a shopkeeper

I graduated from college in the Spring of 1974 with a B.A. in Early Childhood Education (Kindergarten to Sixth grade) and I confidently began mailing out resumés and going on multiple interviews. But 1974 was a time of economic stagnation and I soon became painfully aware that there were no teaching jobs available.

Nonetheless, one of my mother's lady-friends at church arranged an interview for me at the 'Guardian Angel Elementary School' which was supported by the Roman Catholic Parish in the meat-packing district on New York's lower West Side.

At the time the idea of being hired by the New York City Catholic Diocesan Educational System didn't seem an avenue that would make for a happy union. But who could tell? Nothing ventured – nothing gained!

I went to the interview and was immediately offered the job. The offer was as follows – in addition to a truly measly salary, I would be allowed to live rent free in a former nun's 'cell' in the old Convent and I would have kitchen privileges, that is – I could use the Convent kitchen to prepare meals purchased at my own expense. I was warned to be sure to 'label' all the items for identification in the ancient refrigerator and was required to *always* to clean-up afterwards.

Some offer! So I said, "Thank you. I'll think about it," and quickly fled.

Mindful of my frustration, my grandmother asked if I would like to take some time off and visit my friends in Germany at her expense as my graduation present. I can't tell you how happy that made me and I was soon off for a month of fun and recreation in Munich.

I returned from Germany in mid-June, took a deep breath, and went to the Hedland Agency in search of employment. No problem there – it appeared I was a very desirable commodity and was offered a plethora of well-paying positions.

One stood out – the position of Butler for eighty-one year old Alva Bernheimer Gimbel, the widow of Bernard Feustman Gimbel, the former CEO of Gimbel Brothers, Inc.

The interview took place in Mrs. Gimbel's suite in the Hotel Pierre. Seated on a large sofa, both she and her daughter Hope Gimbel Solinger were waiting.

After the usual greetings and introductions were exchanged, I sat across from the two ladies. They had obviously read my resumés and Mrs. Solinger asked one pointed question – "Tell me why, after two years in the Army and having received your college degree, are you considering *this* kind of work?"

Although not prepared for that question I replied,

"The reality is that because of the present economic recession, I couldn't find an acceptable teaching position and therefore had to find a job in a field that I knew well and would enable me to carry on until such time as a teaching position became available."

And I added that I had been offered a less than wonderful teaching position which I hadn't accepted because I couldn't see myself sleeping in a nun's cell and living on a salary that was one step above destitution.

Then I related the reasons I enjoyed being a Butler. I told them how much I relished meeting and interacting with people and how I enjoyed living in the amazing homes of my employers and learning about the art and antiques they lived with.

I continued with my stories of meeting luminaries like – Marjorie Merriweather Post, her daughter Dina and son-in-law Cliff Robertson, the duke and duchess of Windsor, Rose Kennedy, Hildegarde and J. Meyer Schine, Flora Vanderbilt Miller and her cousin, 'Jock" Whitney and a host of others. My stories were magic carpet rides and before I knew it, I once again had a job.

A week later I drove up to The Chieftans' – a thirty-three-room fieldstone manor house on Mrs. Gimbel's two hundred acre estate on King Street in Greenwich, Connecticut. I parked it by the back door, unloaded my luggage, and made my way to the staff dining room where I met my fellow staff members.

The estate consisted of the manor house, a stable, a carriage house, a milk barn and separate chauffeur's quarters. There was also a 1920s in-ground pool that was not used since it was filled with Mrs. Gimbel's son Peter's underwater photography paraphernalia.

'The Chieftans' had an unusually large staff for a woman living alone – a cook, a kitchen aid, a parlor-maid/waitress, a lady's maid, a chauffeur, a houseman, and of course me, the new

Butler. She also had a Social Secretary – Mrs. Stevenson, a charming woman with whom I got along splendidly (for a change.)

The estate had been built for Alfred Whitney Church (an heir to the Borden condensed milk fortune) between 1907 and 1911. The main house was designed by New York architect Augustus Dennis Shepard, Jr. in the Adirondack 'cottage' style. Bernard's father Isaac bought the estate in 1925. Alva and Bernard moved in after his death in 1931.

Bernard's German-Jewish grandfather, Adam Gimbel arrived in the United States from Bavaria in 1835. The ambitious twenty-year old, a novelty peddler in river towns up and down the Mississippi, had the spirit that would enable him to create a fortune. In 1842 he settled in Vincennes, a frontier town on the Wabash River in Indiana where he established a small dry-goods business – grandiosely named 'The Palace of Trade.' The business thrived, due mainly to Adam's 'one price for all' policy – unheard of at the time.

He fathered fourteen children, ten boys and four girls. Seven boys survived to adulthood. In 1889 Adam joined his sons (and Nathan Hamburger – an adopted son,) and opened the first 'Gimbel Brothers' department store in the boomtown of Milwaukee, Wisconsin.

A second 'Gimbel Brothers' opened in Philadelphia in 1894. That year patriarch Adam Gimbel died and his astute second son Isaac (Bernard's father) became president of the family company. In 1909, building on the success of the firm's first two stores, Isaac decided to open a third in New York City. He made Bernard vice-president of 'Gimbel Brothers' and put him in charge of the new store on Herald Square.

On a trip to New York Bernard met Alva Bernheimer, the daughter of a wealthy, socially prominent, German-Jewish family. Unlike New York's other German-Jewish families such as the

Goldmans, Lehmans, Loebs, Seligmans, Sachs, Warbergs, etc., who were primarily bankers, the Bernheimers were in the cotton business. They were nonetheless charter members of the elite, insular group of New York City's Jewish patricians that came to be known as 'Our Crowd.'

The Herald Square store opened in 1910. Alva and Bernard were married on April 4, 1912 in the then five-year old Plaza Hotel. The guests included the elite of New York's German-Jewish society. Alva's sister, Mrs. M. Robert Guggenheim was Matron of Honor. Daniel Guggenheim, Jr. was the flower boy.

In 1922 Bernard suggested to his father and brothers that the family-owned business go public as Gimbel Brothers, Inc. They all agreed. The sale of shares of the new corporation on the New York Stock Exchange provided the firm with capital for expansion. It acquired the two Saks & Company stores in New York. In 1925 the company added the Kaufmann & Baer department store in Pittsburgh.

In 1927 Isaac was thrown from a horse and paralyzed. Bernard succeeded him as president. In 1953 Bruce, Bernard and Alva's eldest son, succeeded his father.

Twenty years later Bruce negotiated the sale of the corporation (then comprised of sixty-nine Gimbels and Saks Fifth Avenue stores) to Brown & Williamson, a subsidiary of the British-American Tobacco Company for $195 million. The last Gimbel store closed in 1987.

During one of my frequent chats with Mrs. Gimbel, she said that 'Our Crowd' was not pleased when she announced her engagement to Bernard. They considered him a – *'shopkeeper.'* What could be worse!

'The Chieftans' evoked another era – a time when elegant dances, parties and large family gatherings were frequent and joyous occasions. The dining room ran the full width of the house. The table when extended, could easily seat eighteen.

A huge portrait of Mrs. Gimbel hung over the massive, ornate fireplace. The portrait by Raymond Constant de Guttman portrays her as a regal and self-reliant woman. Reminiscent of the work of John Singer Sargent she stands erect, perhaps gazing down at a wondrous black-tie dinner party, watching over the now silent festivities of past guests. Her gaze was spellbinding.

The painting fascinated me and I thought,

"What could have been going through her mind as she stood silent, hour after hour, while this masterpiece was being created?"

The thirty-five by sixty-five foot Great Hall seemed right out of a grand nineteenth-century Adirondack lodge. A huge fieldstone fireplace dominated the space. Handmade log roof trusses formed the ceiling. There were several seating areas filled with sturdy, comfortable furniture and lamps and family photos crowded every available horizontal surface.

Bernard and Alva had five children. The first child, Bruce was born in 1913. Non-identical twin girls, Hope and Caral, followed in 1914 and in 1928, identical twin boys, David and Peter were born. David died of cancer in 1957 at age twenty-nine. Peter, his twin was deeply affected by his untimely passing.

In 1956 Peter dove to the wreck of the Andrea Doria, the luxurious Italian ocean liner that recently sank off Nantucket Island after colliding with a smaller Swedish ship – the Stockholm. Peter's photographs of the sunken liner were published in Life Magazine in August of that year.

Captivated by the submerged ship he dove back down five more times to photograph it and he produced two film documentaries about it.

On most weekends while I was at 'The Chieftans,' Peter arrived with his future wife Elga Andersen, a beautiful German film actress and singer. She assisted him in testing his underwater photographic equipment in the pool which was covered with a tarpaulin when they weren't there and therefore, couldn't be enjoyed. They kept to themselves and usually dined out alone.

When Mrs. Gimbel was home alone, she was served breakfast by her personal maid in her bedroom. She had her lunch at numerous locations depending on the weather and events of any given day. Come evening, she would dine from a tray in front of her TV in the Great Hall.

When she had weekend guests (her children, grandchildren and friends,) dinners took place in the dining room. I enjoyed that since it allowed me to display my ability to set up and serve an elegant meal and assuaged my growing boredom.

I tried every trick I could think of in an attempt to create stimulating activities to move the time along. I took an inventory of the Butler's pantry including the china, the linens, the crystal and silver. That occupied a little over three weeks – and once again I was bored. So I explored the *front* of the house in depth. In my last attempt to quell my boredom, I socialized frequently with friends in Westchester and even made a few evening runs down to New York City, but all to no avail.

Looking back at the time in question I honestly believe I made good use of that quiet, low paced lifestyle to allow me to plan my future. Even so, after several weeks of this uninspiring routine, my wanderlust urge resurfaced and 'the writing was on the wall.'

I dealt with this situation until Mrs. Gimbel, wise and compassionate woman that she was, began to hint that perhaps I might be happier with some other employer – one who might have a livelier household routine. So when I gave notice in mid-August, she smiled knowingly and said,

"Hope and I knew that down the line you would be bored here, but I liked you so much, I decided to see if you could make a go of it. But I understand that an intelligent, creative young man such as you needs excitement and challenges. I'm sorry to see you go, but I'm certain you'll soon find a more satisfying position in your chosen profession – teaching."

The Reference she gave me was one of my best.

Chapter Thirteen

The Goldmans

Six Degrees of Separation

Heeding Mrs. Gimbel's advice to pursue my 'chosen' profession, I resumed sending my resumé to and going on interviews at several private schools – to no avail. So I went back to the Hedland agency. I had a choice of options but I chose Mr. and Mrs. Nathan Goldman. There was something about the name that seemed familiar.

The next day I arrived at 778 Park Avenue. The Goldmans were waiting for me in the paneled mahogany library of their floor-through apartment. Mrs. Goldman was seated on the sofa – Mr. Goldman at a large partners desk nearby.

Jacqueline Goldman was a beautiful French woman. Mr. Goldman, seemingly older, deferred to her and she began my interview.

It seemed that the Hedland had provided her not only with a summary of my previous Buttling positions and my growing collection of glowing References but also with my list of requisites. There were however, some added duties that the agency had somehow forgotten to mention to me – I was required to act as their chauffeur from time to time and take care of Mr.

Goldman's clothes as his valet. So I politely asked for a higher salary. They acquiesced and I accepted the position.

It was then, gazing at Mr. Goldman, that I remembered where our paths had crossed in the past.

I was a tall boy at twelve, neat in appearance and quite knowledgeable in the game of golf which my father played regularly with me as his 'caddie.' At that time, my uncle Bud offered to introduce me to friend of his who was the 'caddie master' at the exclusively Jewish, Long Island Golf & Country Club in Glen Oaks. In a short time I became *the* preferred caddie for some of the best 'loops' (rounds of golf) there. Mr. Goldman was one of my 'clients.' Caddies work for tips and Mr. Goldman was always very generous. So I told him that I had once been his caddie.

His reaction was quite positive. He found it amazing that the young boy who had been his caddie in 1958 was now a former Army Medic, a college graduate and had worked for some of the richest families in the country was, by some odd quirk of fate, his new Butler.

Since Mrs. Goldman was French the apartment was furnished with fine 18th century French furniture. By repute, two pieces came from Versailles. I had observed Museum-quality furniture before – principally at Mrs. Post's Hillwood, but I was intrigued by it and since Wednesday was my day off, I decided to explore the nearby Metropolitan Museum of Art where I discovered the collection of Jayne and Charles Wrightsman. I decided to learn everything I could about art and antique furniture. So I began to haunt the Madison Avenue galleries on my day off.

The Goldman's staff in In New York it consisted of three – Anna, their parlor-maid/cook, Sara, the laundress who did not live in, and me. My chauffeuring duties in the city consisted of picking up Mr. Goldman at his office a few times a week. He either taxied to work or walked in good weather in the morning. My so-called 'valet' duties presented no problem – Mr. Goldman was fastidious.

Every weekend we went to the Goldman's country estate on Duck Pond Road in Locust Valley – a five minute drive from the Burden's former home on Piping Rock Road. The estate was called *Bois Jolie* (Pretty Woodlands.) Their house was a thirty-three room, Georgian-style mansion. I drove them there in their Cadillac. It was not a limousine. Anna sat in front with me and the groceries were packed in the car's small trunk.

Each autumn in New York the Goldmans hosted several major fund-raising galas for Jewish charities. The events were lavish cocktail parties or elegant formal dinners. I enjoyed supervising both with competent extra help, of course – but …

I was bored again. And the prospect of spending the long, cold Winter in New York inspired me to go South again – specifically back to Palm Beach.

I believed my boredom non-apparent, but Mrs. Goldman surprised me one evening by asking if there was the possibility that I was thinking of leaving them in the near future. I said yes. I told her that while I enjoyed working for them but I couldn't deal with a New York City winter when Palm Beach beckoned.

The following week I went back to the Hedland agency and reviewed a list of potential employers. All were Palm Beach old money and lived on either Ocean- or Lake Worth-facing properties.

I had also increased my list of requests.

1. A minimum staff of five.

2. Preferably an older couple.

3. A higher salary.

I was right – the only way to get ahead in this 'profession' was to change jobs – frequently.

Mrs. Goldman's gave me a superb hand-written Reference which said that I had performed my duties as 'Maître d'hôtel' perfectly.

Chapter Fourteen

Blanche Paley Levy

J&B on the rocks with a splash

The Hedland found me another job quickly – but this time it was my *perfect* job. My interview took place in the U.N. Towers. It was conducted by two of my future employer's close New York friends. The couple read my *all* my References and asked the usual questions. All my requirements, including a raise in salary, had been negotiated ahead of time by the Hedland.

I obviously impressed the couple because they phoned my potential new employer in Palm Beach. To my surprise, their conversation took place in my presence. But it consisted of mainly yes's and no's and a few moments later they handed me the phone.

A cultivated, finishing-school voice inquired if I had ever worked for Mrs. Robert R. Young in Newport. I answered yes. She asked me to please stay on the line as she was giving the phone to someone who had an important question for me.

"Hello" another female voice said, "Thomas? Is that really you?"

"Yes, I'm really Thomas," I answered, a bit confused.

"The same Thomas I danced with in Mrs. Young's pantry all those years ago in Newport?"

"Yes," I answered, instantly recognizing Lorraine's sweet, southern drawl. "I can't believe it's you Lorraine. How are you?"

"I'm fine, just *fine!* When I heard that someone by the name of Thomas Gardner might be coming down here to be our Butler, I got so excited I couldn't wait to find out if it could be the same Thomas I remembered. The idea that it just might be you brought back such fun memories. I told Mrs. Levy all about you and we laughed and laughed, especially at that story about Mrs. Young's missing clapper and that horrible Valdemar. Wasn't he a hoot? Well, I tell you Thomas – you just come on down here – we're gonna have a funky good time for sure!

Of course I accepted the position and I was on my way to Palm Beach in my red Volkswagen in January.

Seven years had passed since I left Mar-a-Lago and everything changed. The seven mile drive from the Florida Turnpike to downtown West Palm Beach was much wider and busier than I could have ever envisioned. There were new shopping malls and many new gated communities – each vying for attention with pretentious names, Versailles-style fountains, elaborate plantings and full-grown Royal Palms flanking their entrances.

It seemed that West Palm Beach had morphed into an ersatz Palm Beach. And the traffic! I might as well have been back in New York at rush hour.

Nevertheless when I crossed over the Royal Palm Bridge and entered the *real* Palm Beach, I felt a moment of excitement sweep over me. A new adventure was about to begin!

I drove by Mar-a-Lago, now unoccupied except for a small maintenance staff. The villa, that had so pulsated with life when Mother reigned supreme – was now an empty, unwanted relic of the past.

The villa was offered to the state of Florida for use as a center for advanced scholars but Florida officials, dissuaded by the high cost of maintenance turned it down. Then in 1968 the villa was offered to the federal government as the Winter White House, but for that same reason and the fact that the villa was a security risk (arriving and departing planes to and from the West Palm Beach airport flew over-head) the government also turned it down and gave it to the Post Foundation.

A few minutes later I entered the drive of 1830 South Ocean Boulevard, the Palm Beach residence of my new employers – Dr. and Mrs. Leon Levy. Following the sign that read 'Service Entrance,' I drove by a towering wall of expertly-clipped, green ficus hedges then stopped in a large courtyard, landscaped with flowering shrubs and Royal Palms.

There was a large green and white striped canvas carport sheltering a one year old Cadillac El Dorado. A handsome three-car garage was nearby.

I parked my Volkswagen under the striped canopy next to the Cadillac, got out and stretched. Breathing in the soft, early evening freshness, I knew that this would be a wonderful Palm Beach season.

I entered the house and found my way to the Butler's pantry. There stood Lorraine looking much as she had when I last saw her in Newport all those years ago. She exclaimed,

"As I live and breathe – it's really you!"

We chatted as we walked through the large kitchen into the staff dining room where dinner was finishing up. The Levy's had a large staff – nine, counting me.

They were all there and Lorraine made the introductions. I met her husband Danny, the chauffeur, Mr. Levy's valet George, beautiful Brazilian Edith, Mrs. Levy's personal lady's maid and occasionally my reluctant assistant as my waitress, Sophie, the kitchen aid, Flora, the parlor-maid and Karl, the inept houseman with an awful, shoe-polish-black toupée. They all greeted me and silently sat evaluating me – the new arrival. And, once again I was the youngest.

I commented on the Cadillac parked outside and learned that it belonged to Louise, Mrs. Levy's personal secretary who had her own apartment in West Palm Beach. Louise used one of the two guest room suites as her daytime office. Lorraine and Danny were married and lived in their own Spanish-style home a block from Lake Worth in West Palm Beach.

A born mechanic, Danny's responsibility as chauffeur was driving Doctor and Mrs. Levy, and keeping their Rolls Royce, Chrysler Imperial and Chevrolet estate-wagon in top condition.

The house had a large, beautifully landscaped swimming pool that the Levys never used. A large, mature gardenia bush stood guard at each corner. The strong, intoxicating scent from their pure white flowers was truly overwhelming at times, especially on sultry, warm evenings.

On the north side of the pool, just off the huge living room was a terrace protected by an awning. It was the perfect place for luncheons or quiet gazing out at Lake Worth. On the south side of the pool were two guest bedrooms which were separated by a cozy, open logia and were rarely used – since there were never any overnight guests.

The next morning I met the Levys. Doctor and Mrs. Levy had finished their breakfasts in their individual separate dressing room suites. Louise asked me to join her in the library at ten o'clock to meet them. They were both in their seventies. Mrs. Levy appeared to be the taller of the two – or perhaps her bouffant, grey-streaked hairdo made her appear so.

She wore a beautiful outfit by Martha and earrings and a bracelet by her favorite jeweler, David Webb. Doctor was also a David Webb aficionado and had an impressive collection of at least a dozen sets of the designer's cuff-links.

They were both very pleasant and not at all pretentious. They greeted me warmly and said they hoped I would be happy working for them. I thanked them and told them how pleased I was with my accommodations.

A dentist by trade, Doctor Leon Levy founded WCAU, a local Philadelphia radio station in 1927. At that time a new radio network, the United Independent Broadcasters (UIB) was being organized by two promoters, Arthur Judson and George Coats. Searching out local radio stations to join the new network, Coats approached Dr. Levy and WCAU became UIB's first affiliate.

'Doctor' agreed to provide the network with ten hours of broadcasting for five hundred dollars per week. Eleven other local stations from Chicago to Boston soon joined in. However, due to the soaring costs of transmitting the broadcasts and the payments to their growing number of affiliates, Judson and Coats were badly in debt.

Consequently, the Columbia Phonographic Company agreed to invest one-hundred-sixty-three-thousand dollars in UIB, with a condition that the network be renamed the Columbia Phonographic Broadcasting System (CPBS.)

Unfortunately for Judson and Coats, their inability to attract paying sponsors and the resulting financial drain forced the Columbia Phonographic Company to withdraw their offer.

Judson appealed to 'Doctor' (who was well connected with Philadelphia's moneyed Jewish community) for help and one Jerome Louchheim agreed to re-capitalize the company. 'Doctor' and his lawyer brother Isaac (Ike) Levy decided to invest as well and Louchheim and the Levy brothers took control of the company – Louchheim of course had the largest share.

The new owners changed the company name to the Columbia Broadcasting System (CBS). In the meantime 'Doctor' married Blanche Paley, the sister of one of WCAU's advertising clients – William S. (Bill) Paley.

Business was not good and Louchheim soon lost interest in CBS. In 1928 'Doctor' informed his new brother-in-law Bill of Louchheim's desire by to sell his shares of CBS. Convinced that radio advertising was the wave of the future, Bill purchased forty-one percent of the network for four-hundred-seventeen-thousand dollars, money he had received from the sale of his stock in his family's business – the Congress Cigar Company.

Other family members bought enough stock to give the Paleys control of CBS. On September 26, 1928, two days before his twenty-seventh birthday, Bill became president of the company.

Under his direction CBS became one of the most successful radio broadcasting networks in the world.

The Paley family saga began in Czarist Russia. The false rumors that the Jews were responsible for the 1881 assassination of Czar Alexander II, fueled a series of government-sanctioned Pogroms (riots) against Jewish communities.

In 1882, the new Czar, Alexander III enacted the anti-Semitic 'May Laws' which severely and negatively impacted Jewish freedom in the Russian Empire. Jews were forced to leave the countryside and migrate to large towns and cities where strict quotas limited their educational opportunities and many professions were prohibited to them.

The Pogroms eventually ended but an anti-Semitic press kept the threat of reprisals alive. Konstantin Pobedonostsev, the Czar's friend and mentor, and the leader of the Holy Synod – the *governing body of the Russian Orthodox Church, made Russia's position clear – Jews could leave Russia or convert to Russian Orthodoxy or die.*

Not surprisingly more than two million chose to leave. Some went to Palestine but the majority emigrated to England, Ireland, South Africa and the United States.

In 1886 Ukrainian-born Samuel Paley arrived in Chicago. After working several smalltime jobs and learning English, he found work in a cigar factory as a lector – a man who amused the workers by reading books and periodicals aloud as they performed the mind-deadening work of rolling leaf tobacco into cigars.

Samuel, fascinated by the cigar business and its remunerative possibilities, learned all there was to know about the growing and blending of tobacco and the manufacture of cigars. He was soon promoted to a roller – and then to a blender.

Entrepreneurial Samuel opened his own cigar factory and shop in Chicago in 1896 called Samuel Paley & Company, but soon renamed it the 'Congress Cigar Company.' The company's first cigar brand was dubbed 'La Palina' – a play on the family name.

In 1898 twenty-three year old Samuel married another Jewish immigrant from the Ukraine, Goldie Drell. The couple's first child William was born in 1901. Their daughter Blanche arrived in 1905.

Labor problems prompted Samuel to move the company to Philadelphia in about 1920. By that time he was a multimillionaire. Samuel and Goldie's son 'Bill' joined the company as the production and advertising manager after graduating from Philadelphia's Wharton School of Business. He earned fifty-thousand dollars annually.

The cigar company sponsored a radio show on Dr. Levy's WCAU called 'The La Palina Hour.' In six months the commercials had increased cigar sales by one hundred and fifty percent – potent proof of the power of radio advertising.

The cigar business thrived and was ultimately traded on the New York Stock Exchange. In 1928 the family sold two hundred shares of their company's stock to the American Tobacco Company for almost fourteen million dollars. This provided Bill Paley with enough capital to buy CBS.

Doctor and Blanche married in 1927 and moved into the prestigious *Rittenhouse Plaza* building in Philadelphia. Blanche gave birth to their son Robert in 1931. Shortly thereafter the young family moved from the duplex apartment on Rittenhouse Square to 'White Corners' – a Federal-style mansion on the northeast corner of Henry Avenue and School House Lane.

In 1937 the Levy's adopted a daughter named Lyn. They disinherited her when she married Chuck Barris, the host of the Gong Show, against their will. Louise instructed me to never, under any circumstances bring up her name.

Like the Schines, the Levys had simple taste in food – broiled chicken or fish almost every night as Mrs. Levy had digestive issues.

They rarely had formal, sit-down lunches. Mrs. Levy, if she lunched at all, would have it in her private, sitting/dressing room off the master bedroom. Doctor lunched alone as well – often at poolside by the covered terrace. At times Danny drove him to one of the cafés in the Poinciana Mall. There was little activity in the house until the cocktail hour, which was followed by their uninspiring dinner service.

They really had no need of a Butler and there was no need to assume any additional tasks such as valet or chauffeur as I had done on many of my previous locations even though I had been initially hired as 'Butler.'

The Levys were horse people. Sometime in the 1940s Doctor and his brother-in-law Bill Paley developed 'Jaclyn Stables' that owned, bred and raced thoroughbreds. The name 'Jaclyn' was an acronym of the Levy's children's names – son Robert (Jack) and daughter Lyn.

During the Palm Beach season, whenever one of their horses was racing at the Hialeah Park Race Track near Fort Lauderdale – Doctor and Mrs. Levy attended. She accompanied him under duress as she didn't want to be too far from the security of her home.

Several weeks into the season Mrs. Levy and I reached a level of mutual comfort. This fostered – prior to Doctor's arrival in the library at the cocktail hour – frank and often revealing, conversations when we were by ourselves. Mrs. Levy had a good sense of humor and was well grounded, despite, or perhaps because of, the ups and downs that life had given her.

One afternoon as we awaited Doctor's usually late cocktail hour arrival, Mrs. Levy began to relate her tale of young 'Miss Paley.' Sipping the first of her evening's J&B cocktails, Mrs. Levy related her experiences at one of the East Coast's finest finishing schools for girls – Miss Porter's in Farmington, Connecticut. She said her years at 'Farmington' were trying inasmuch as she had to hide her Jewish origins. She told me she alluded to be Episcopalian since Farmington was restricted – Catholics and Jews were not openly welcomed. But money however, (sometimes) has a way of overcoming certain barriers.

Mrs. Levy said she was sure that during her years at Miss Porter's there were several other Jewish girls there but they hid the fact – even from each other. She told me she was upset by the oft-asked question, 'What kind of name is Paley? To this she said she would reply, 'Paley is of

Russian origin,' and then skillfully move the conversation in another direction. According to her the reply 'usually' put an end to further inquiry.

She joked that one of the reasons she decided to marry 'Doctor' was a direct result of those nosey, Miss Porter girls. She said with her married name now being Levy, the annoying question as to her religious persuasion would once and for all *be put to rest* .

She went on to say that her brother Bill seemed to deal with this 'problem' in another fashion. As it turned out Bill's first and second wife were *not* of the Jewish faith, but – ultra-W.A.S.P. – and highly-ranked in the Social Register.

Mrs. Levy opined that Bill was not too happy being Jewish and his yearning for W.A.S.P. acceptance was the reason he married out of the faith – twice.

Bill's first wife was Dorothy Hart Hearst the former wife of William Randolph Hearst, Jr. They married in 1932 and had two children. They divorced in 1947. Later that year Bill married the beautiful, divorced socialite, Barbara "Babe" Cushing Mortimer. They also had two children. Bill is buried alongside Babe in the Memorial Cemetery of St. John's Episcopal Church in Laurel Hollow, Long Island.

One warm February afternoon, a vintage Silver Cloud, Rolls Royce pulled into the drive. Earlier in the day, I was informed that two of Mrs. Levy's friends would arrive for an afternoon cocktail. The entry of the Rolls into the front drive triggered a buzzer that sounded in the pantry and staff dining room. Alerted, I made my way to the front door and greeted the arriving guests.

The woman, still beautiful at seventy-seven was Mrs. Margaret Majer Kelly, a neighbor from both Philadelphia and Palm Beach. The burly driver was none other than 'Big Daddy' Flannigan, the CEO of the eponymous chain of cocktail lounges and package liquor stores in South Florida.

Mrs. Kelly was born in Germany and was a former model. She was the widow of John (Jack) Kelly, the son of Irish immigrants and an Olympic gold medalist. Jack started out as a bricklayer, but later founded a thriving brickwork contracting company in Philadelphia. And yes – Margaret and Jack were the proud parents of – Her Serene Highness, Princess Grace of Monaco.

I led them to the poolside terrace where Mrs. Levy, her J&B on the rocks and her ubiquitous cigarette waited. They had three 'tea parties' that season. Their conversations ran from politics to family matters to the changing standards of the times. Excepting these few social contacts, Mrs. Levy was a lonely woman. She was convinced that Doctor was having an affair. Only Danny the chauffeur knew where 'Doctor' spent his afternoons – and he was extremely tight-lipped.

I've already mentioned the Levy's love of David Webb jewelry. But they also loved the designer's *objets d'art*. They owned two that accompanied them to Palm Beach in the winter and Philadelphia in the summer. One was a large, solid-gold box in the shape of a frog and the other was a solid-gold, diamond encrusted palm tree in a latticework basket.

In Palm Beach they were both kept in the living room on two long parsons tables behind two matching sofas. In Philadelphia they were in the upstairs dining room. The palm tree was on the dining table, the frog box on the cocktail table in front of the love seat.

One afternoon in Palm Beach Mrs. Levy called me on the intercom. She was hysterical.

"Thomas," she shouted, "Someone stole the Webb!"

"Your jewelry's been stolen? Should I call the police?"

"No, no, no – the box, the frog box – it's gone. It's been stolen."

I hadn't realized that the frog was by David Webb and was totally unaware of its intrinsic value. But I had noticed earlier that the box appeared dull and instead of asking Flora to attend to it, I took it back into the pantry for an ammonia wash. Then I poured myself a cup of coffee and sat in the staff dining room to read the gossipy, always fascinating, Palm Beach Shiny Sheet.

So I said with relief,

"The frog is here in the pantry. I cleaned it and was about to return it to the living room. I'll bring it right in."

A few days later Louise asked if I would join her at the Colony Hotel on Saturday night for cocktails and dancing.

Lorraine had mentioned that I loved to dance to her and I accepted eagerly. The Colony was at the time a boutique hotel south of Worth Avenue. It was a well-known retreat for Palm Beach Society. Even the duke and duchess of Windsor had resided there in years past.

Louise was a knock-out that night. She looked like a fabulous Las Vegas showgirl. We had several drinks, danced a lot and left just after midnight. Driving back, I finally raised the courage to ask her why she sun-bathed almost every day at the Levy's pool. She said,

"It makes Doctor happy. He finds me a very attractive woman."

"So Mrs. Levy could be right about Doctor's *affair*," I thought. But I never mentioned it to her.

A week or so later I was in the pantry reading the Shiny Sheet when the house phone rang. I answered it and said, "The Levy residence. How may I help you?"

It was a man's voice and he had an odd question. He wanted to know the width of all the doorjambs from the front entrance to the living room. I knew of no scheduled furniture delivery so I was suspicious, and asked,

"Why?"

The voice said that a strawberry pink-speckled poinsettia plant was due to be delivered that afternoon. The plant, he said, would be *unwrapped* to protect it from being 'bruised.' I asked his phone number and said I would call him back with the measurements he requested.

I called Louise to see what was up. She told me that Bill and Babe Paley were planning an afternoon stopover next week in Palm Beach. They often stopped to visit his (and Mrs. Levy's) mother Goldie Paley. They were traveling to their house 'Round Hill' in Jamaica and were flying down on the CBS jet. Bill wanted to stop in Palm Beach to see Doctor, Blanche, and his mother Goldie who had her own house nearby.

A luncheon at the Levys was scheduled for that day. I was informed that there would be six for lunch – Goldie Paley, Doctor and Mrs. Levy, Bill and Babe Paley and an unidentified guest. Louise said the poinsettia was a holiday gift from Bill and Babe.

When the plant arrived my first reaction was that it was grown for a Cecil B. de Mille mega-movie production. It was more like a poinsettia *tree* than a plant.

Where to put it?

Lorraine thought it would look best in front of the floor-to-ceiling plate glass window at the far end of the entrance gallery. What added to the total impact of that location was that both the swimming pool and two of the four large gardenia plants which could be seen through the glass and would serve as appropriate backdrops for the impressive poinsettia. So we put it there.

The house was always ready to entertain but Mrs. Levy wanted to pull out all the stops this time. I put everyone to work to made sure the house could pass a 'white-glove' inspection – that is, groomed to a fault.

Two days before the Paley's arrival, two saleswomen from Martha (*the* Palm Beach/New York fashion emporium for ladies of a certain age) arrived with a staggering selection of elegant outfits for Mrs. Levy's private viewing. Mrs. Levy purchased a truly sensational garment. It was altered for her and delivered the next day.

The visit would begin with cocktails on the terrace followed by luncheon in the dining room. I rose early that day to set the wheels in motion. The floral centerpiece arrived at eight-thirty. An hour later I finished arranging the table with Mrs. Levy's best china and silver.

The menu was simple – an avocado and shrimp salad followed by broiled red snapper in hot lemon butter sauce garnished with boiled new potatoes. Lorraine's fabulous peach cobbler would finish off what we knew would be a fantastic, yet understated lunch.

Goldie Paley arrived at about noon. She was beautifully dressed and coiffed. I led her to the terrace where Doctor and Mrs. Levy were waiting. A soft, pleasant breeze from Lake Worth set the tone and drinks were offered. For Goldie Paley an iced tea was fine, for Doctor – a glass of chardonnay, and for Mrs. Levy – her usual J&B on the rocks with a splash.

Fifteen minutes later the buzzer alert in the pantry sounded and a long, black limousine pulled into the drive and stopped at the front door. The chauffeur opened the rear door and Bill and Babe Paley alighted. Then a short, blonde man in a white suit with a long scarf around his neck hopped out. I couldn't believe my eyes. It was Truman Capote!

The Paleys met Mr. Capote in 1955. Film producer David O. Selznick and his wife, Jennifer Jones were invited to spend a weekend at the Paley's house in Jamaica. Selznick asked if a good friend could join them. Bill and Babe consented and the five flew to Jamaica on the CBS jet.

Babe Paley and Truman Capote met for the first time on that flight and bonded immediately. Bill didn't mind – he knew their relationship would never be anything more than platonic. He too liked Mr. Capote and always called him 'Tru-boy.'

From that time on the odd trio were constant companions. Mr. Capote spent long periods of time with them at their houses in Jamaica, the Bahamas and Long Island. He sailed with them on their yacht and accompanied them to Europe.

I escorted the new arrivals to the terrace. After the usual greetings and air kisses were exchanged, Bill Paley asked for a scotch and soda, his wife, some Perrier. Mr. Capote, with a wink and a smile, requested a 'light' scotch. I don't think it was his first drink that day.

I slipped off to the pantry to prepare the drinks. Everyone, staff wise, was excited by Mr. Capote's appearance. Having assembled the requested drinks, I placed them on a serving tray and made my way back to the terrace.

By then Babe was chatting with Blanche, Goldie with son Bill, and Truman with Doctor. I overheard Doctor mention that he had just finished reading *Mojave* in the recent issue of Esquire Magazine. *Mojave* is a short story purportedly excerpted from Truman's long-anticipated novel, *Answered Prayers*.

Doctor said he had enjoyed reading the tale of an aging stripper who marries a blind man, cheats on him, steals his money and house trailer and finally abandons him in the Mojave Desert. Not having read the work, I found the plot, as outlined by Doctor, quite bizarre.

Then Doctor asked the question that everyone was eager to have answered, "Truman, is *Answered Prayers* finished yet?"

Capote, in his signature, annoyingly high-pitched voice, laughed and turning to be sure everyone was listening said in his unforgettable way,

"Leon, like everyone else, you'll simply just have to wait and see." A look of annoyance flashed over Doctor's face and a sense of confrontation was now in the air.

Cocktails finished, the group made their way inside to the dining room. The seating arrangement was as follows – Doctor was seated at the head of the table, Mrs. Levy at the other end. Mr. Capote sat to her left, Babe Paley next to him and Bill Paley and his mother opposite both.

Because of the larger than usual number dining I was assisted by Edith. Desert was being served and Mr. Capote once again signaled for another drink when I heard Mrs. Levy shriek,

"Jacques! Get out!"

Jacques, Mrs. Levy's off-white miniature poodle – a fluff-ball with the heart and spirit of a racehorse was making his unexpected entrance into the dining room. He had several interesting routines in his repertoire. If the door to Mrs. Levy's private quarters (where he was frequently an unhappy prisoner) happened to be left just slightly ajar, Jacques would escape.

Once having gained his temporary freedom he would race through the entire length of the *front* of the house (consisting of the Levy's bedroom complex, the library, the massive forty-foot living room, the front entry gallery and the dining room). His ultimate destination was the *back* of the house where he was certain to find someone to give him a treat.

That day however he chose a different route since not only was the door to Mrs. Levy's private quarters ajar but also the living room door to the terrace and pool complex. Jacque seized the moment and jumped into the shallow end of the pool, paddled around for a time, and shaking off the excess water, went in search of some long-buried treasure (perhaps a bone) at the base of one of the large gardenia bushes. The result of his venture left Jacques covered with mud.

On hearing the guests' voices, Jacques made his entrance from poolside to the dining room leaving a long, unsightly trail of muddy water.

Reacting quickly, I picked up Jacques as quickly as possible and the room slowly returned to normal. In the end it was the Edward Field's carpet that took the most abuse.

A glance at the clock revealed that the time had come to end the lunch. The CBS jet had a short window of departure from the airport that couldn't be missed. There were the usual hugs and kisses and good wishes for the coming holidays and New Year and then – all were gone.

That evening at dinner, Doctor commented,

"Blanche, luncheon was the most exciting and amusing event I can remember taking place here, but honestly – a little bit of Capote goes a long way. I don't know what your brother and sister-in-law see in him. That guy has an agenda."

Doctor wasn't surprised when Capote, in an act of utter self-destruction, alienated Bill and Babe (arguably his most faithful friends) forever a while later. Here's how he did it –

Capote often touted *Answered Prayers* as his literary masterpiece but he never finished it. However, in November 1975 Esquire Magazine published an excerpt entitled *La Côte Basque 1965*. The Paleys learned of it on their return from Jamaica.

The episode is set in Henri Soulé's East 55th Street eatery, *La Côte Basque* – the preferred oasis of the beautiful New York society women Capote idolized – his so-called 'Swans.' (Babe Paley was of course, one of them.)

In it P.B. Jones (a thinly-disguised Capote) lunches with Lady Ina Coolbirth. During the course of their champagne-logged meal, Lady Ina dishes several well-known women socialites then lunching in the restaurant and rehashes a twenty-year-old society killing and, prodded by the presence of the wife of a former New York governor, relates the tale of an adulterous, one night stand between said wife and a handsome, wealthy Jewish executive longing for W.A.S.P. acceptance.

Anyone who knew Bill and Babe made the obvious association. The Paleys never spoke to Capote again.

I saw Truman seven months later at the Blue Moon, a popular bar/disco in Southampton, New York. It was well past midnight and he had passed out on a banquette near the entrance. Being a genius often comes with a heavy price tag.

One cocktail hour in late March Mrs. Levy arrived in the library as I was preparing her usual panacea – a J&B on the rocks with a splash of water. When she was seated I offered it to her on a small silver tray. As she reached for the drink she stopped, stared down at my shoes, looked up at me and said,

"You know Thomas, I've had many Butlers in my time but none have ever worn Gucci loafers." Mrs. Levy and I, at this point, had reached a level of mutual candor when we were alone together – so I said,

"Well, Mrs. Levy, I don't believe Guccis are *only* for the very rich."

"I agree," she replied laughing. Sometime later I received a gift certificate from Gucci on Worth Avenue – enough for several pair of those wonderful loafers.

At the end of the Palm Beach Winter season we all moved to 'White Corners,' the Levy's home in Germantown – a charming village just a few miles from downtown Philadelphia. It is akin to living in the country. There, Doctor and Mrs. Levy lived a simple, non-social lifestyle. The staff joked that the Levys worked for us – there was so little for us to do.

'White Corners' is a three-story Federal-style mansion at the corner of Henry Avenue and School House Lane. Doctor and Mrs. Levy bought it in the 1930s shortly after their son Robert was born. It was built between 1914 and 1920 for Miss Viola Carstairs of the Philadelphia-based Carstairs Brothers Distilling Company. (Their trademark was a Black Seal balancing a beach ball on its nose).

Edith and Sophie occupied staff quarters on the third floor. Lorraine lived with her husband Danny in an apartment over the large, three-car garage. Louise stayed in her high-rise apartment near Main Line. George had his own apartment a ten-minute drive from the house.

Doctor and Mrs. Levy gave me their son Robert's second-floor bedroom suite complete with a superb Art Deco bathroom. I loved it.

The Levys of course had their own master bedroom suite with two separate dressing rooms and baths. There were two guest bedrooms, one of which had been converted into the 'upstairs' dining room.

A tennis court and a swimming pool were at the far end of the property. Both were never used. In the 1950s Blanche built a more convenient swimming pool outside the library's French double doors.

All the staff cars were required to park in the alley on the North side of the house instead of on the drive facing School House Lane. I kept my white Lincoln Continental, a gift from my parents there, along with Louise's Cadillac El Dorado and George's four-year-old Lincoln.

Danny had a nineteen-sixties Ford Fairlane which somehow found a space in the garage next to the Rolls, the Chrysler Imperial and the house station-wagon.

One cocktail hour I overheard Mrs. Levy tell Doctor that she thought the staff had better and more luxurious cars than they had. Well, with the exception of their Rolls, it was true!

We also had better and more interesting meals. Lorraine prepared superb buffet lunches and dinners for us every day while Doctor and Mrs. Levy had their usual broiled fish or chicken with boiled potatoes and green vegetables.

When Samuel Paley died in 1965, Goldie Paley moved to 4200 Henry Avenue. The one-level 'Hollywood ranch' had been built for Doctor's brother Ike and his wife. It was a seven-thousand-square-foot Art Deco mansion with twelve-foot ceilings and nine bathrooms. I thought it a bit too much for a ninety-year old widow, but it was a short walk from 'White Corners.'

However, Goldie Paley did not walk anywhere outside her home. That was the reason that all the staff cars were required to park in the alley on the North side of the house. When she decided to visit her daughter Blanche she would arrive, often unannounced, with her car and driver. So the drive on the School House Lane frontage was *never* used for parking.

On one of her impromptu visits, Mrs. Paley asked me if I would like to play poker with her – for money, of course. I said yes and she asked me to come to her house the next afternoon. Mrs. Levy instructed me to watch her closely – 'Mother cheats,' she laughingly told me.

Surrounded by her excellent paintings in her impressive studio we played for nickels and dimes. I had played a lot of poker in my Army days and was quite proficient, but I thought if I won too often Mrs. Paley might get upset so I decided to throw a few games. No need – she was a Poker-Shark. On average, I lost two out of every three games.

At one time Doctor and his brother-in-law Bill Paley were involved in breeding and racing thoroughbred horses and so a section of White Corners' basement had been designed to resemble a 'Polo Lounge.' The space was like being on board one of the great 1930s ocean liners. A series of gouaches by the Art Deco artist John Vassos hung on the walls. In 1933 Vassos painted three murals for Doctor's radio station – WCAU.

The bar was always stocked, the stemware always sparkled – but sadly, the space was never used – except by me. I often found myself slipping away on quiet afternoons to that magic room – sitting, gazing at the gouaches, imagining all the conversations, the deals, the dreams that must have taken place within its walls.

I still had one last wisdom tooth. The previous three had been extracted in the Army. When the fourth announced its presence, I informed Doctor who was a dentist by profession, and had kept connections in the field even though he no longer practiced.

Doctor made a phone call and the problem was solved. Not only did the Levy's pick up the dentist's bill but they also insisted that I spend the next two days in bed. That event brought back memories of Hildegarde Schine – who had paid for my 1967 surgery in the Gloversville Hospital.

Working at the Levys was easy with little or no pressure but it had no future and once again, I was bored. They were in their late seventies and Mrs. Levy was in poor health. I could be out of a job at any moment so I decided to leave at the end of that summer.

I wanted to give Mrs. Levy time to replace me. When I told her that I would not be returning to Palm Beach for the Winter season she seemed sad, but understanding.

Chapter Fifteen

Red Alert

I took the train from Philadelphia to New York and moved back into my parent's home. A week later I went to the Hedland. They had several new listings for Buttling positions. My first interview would take place in the General Motors Building on Madison Avenue.

When I stepped off the elevator on the fortieth floor I thought I had entered a time warp. The huge office was in startling contrast to the contemporary building that housed it. When I entered the private office of the company's president, my next potential employer, I was reminded of my grandmother's living room. It had Chinese-style rice wallpaper hand-painted with butterflies and birds. The curtains and fringed sofas were in ivory color satin. There were Louis XV-style chairs covered with Aubusson tapestry and elaborate nineteenth-century gilt bronze French candelabra made into lamps.

Seated behind a Louis XVI desk was a smallish woman in her late sixties.

"Please sit down Thomas," she said.

I did. She continued,

"Thomas, I've read your resumés and I must say I'm impressed. I know your three Florida ladies well and I'm especially fond of Hildegarde Schine. But let me be frank. I'm sure you are the perfect Butler and that in a short time my homes would be running beautifully, but I feel that if I hired you I would soon learn that someone, perhaps one of my friends or house guests, would try to lure you away by offering you more money. If you decided to leave I would have to endure this whole process all over again."

I thought for a moment and replied,

"Madam, I am an honorably discharged Army veteran and a college graduate. I am also a principled man and I assure you that I would never walk out on you in the middle of the season. Moreover, in the unlikely event that someone would try to lure me away with the promise of more money – I would not accept their offer."

She leaned forward in her chair and said,

"Thomas, I'm going to talk to you like a Jewish mother. You're obviously an intelligent young man and I don't believe this line of work is in your best interest. It's a job for a lazy man and in the end, it will lead nowhere. My advice to you is to find something, anything that you're passionate about and learn everything you can about that field. Then enter it at the bottom, make as many personal contacts as you can and then drive yourself relentlessly until you reach the top – just as I did. There's so much opportunity in this great country for a young man like you. Don't waste it."

I left her office, not hired but with a new insight as to what I was doing with my life and the choices that were before me. I had mixed feelings. On one hand, I enjoyed the freedom afforded me by being a Butler – the excitement of seeing new places and meeting new people – and being surrounded by and responsible for their wonderful art and antique collections. And yet, this small powerhouse of a lady said things for my benefit that I can never forget.

I sincerely reflected on Estée Lauder's sage advice and eventually took it. But at that moment in time, I really needed a job – so once more it was back to the Hedland.

Summer was imminent, and I had decided that I didn't want a position in *hot* New York City. Southampton and Newport were possibilities, but when the Hedland proposed a Butler's position in Saratoga Springs, New York, my choice was made. Saratoga Springs! What could have been more perfect?

Chapter Sixteen

Off to the races

My second interview took place in the office of Mr. Ogden Phipps at 245 Park Avenue. Neither Mr. nor Mrs. Phipps were present. My interviewer was Mrs. Phipps's secretary Alice Hedinger. We discussed the position and since the Hedland had not informed her of my usual list of demands, I stated them. She smiled and said that the Phipps house in Saratoga Springs was not a great mansion with large staff quarters, but the loft-like apartment over the garage was found to be satisfactory for the male staff. She said that I would have Sunday morning time off for church and have access to the house station-wagon. But, as far as medical insurance was concerned, she looked at me and said, "Not possible."

However, I needed the job and the salary was good and I was intrigued by Saratoga Springs, so I accepted.

Saratoga Springs is named for its natural mineral springs. It began as the summer campground for the Mohawk and Iroquois Indian tribes who called the area 'Sarachtogue.' Its various waters, known for their distinctive tastes ranging from natural to sulfurous were thought to have restorative powers.

As early as the eighteenth century, seekers of health (and immortality) visited Saratoga Springs to drink and/or bathe in its waters. By the late-nineteenth, European-style mineral water spas had become very fashionable in the United States

In 1863 the Saratoga Race Course opened and gambling soon became an added Saratoga Springs attraction.

Lured by mineral water, horse racing, gambling and its proximity to New York City, society and visiting dignitaries flocked to Saratoga Springs in large numbers. Luxurious hotels and spas proliferated.

I arrived on a sunny day in June l976 on the same bus as Mrs. Phipps's new male chef René who was from Martinique and would soon be my roommate.

Mrs. Phipps's gardener/caretaker, a dark-haired young man named Jim, picked us up at the bus station in the house estate wagon. It was a short trip to 717 North Broadway.

Unlike the estates in Old Westbury, Locust Valley or Southampton – the Saratoga society of the 1880s opted to build their summer homes *in town* on North Broadway – a wide avenue lined with massive, ancient trees and Victorian mansions set on manicured lawns. North Broadway is so unique that in 1979 it was recognized as a historic district and listed on the National Register of Historic Places.

The Phipps house was set back approximately fifty feet from the street and sat on a slight rise. It was a refurbished Queen Anne Victorian beauty – resplendent beyond its original owners' dreams. It had a three-quarter wrap-around porch and a porte-cochère. A graveled carriage drive and a footpath led to a massive front door.

The interior was decorated by the team of Robert Denning and Vincent Fourcade, Mrs. Phipps's preferred designers who also supplied her with eighteenth-century French and English furniture and *objets d'art*. Denning & Fourcade also designed the Phipps' homes in New York City, Florida and South Carolina.

The first floor, replete with potted palms consisted of a suite of opulent rooms. After entering through the impressive front door, a parlor of Victorian splendor welcomed the guests. It led to a large dining room and a most inviting library. The second floor bedrooms were equally luxuriant. Backstage was of course, simpler. The Butler's pantry however, could accommodate a Regiment. There were three female staff members.

Mrs. Phipps's personal lady's maid Marianne shared an attic room with Frances, the parlor-maid/waitress. Jenny, a Skidmore College student was a temporary parlor-maid and commuted to and from her dormitory on her bicycle.

René and I were the only two live-in men. We were both housed in the large, airy, loft-like quarters on the second floor of the barn-like garage. It was actually quite nice since it was distant from the main house and extremely quiet. The bathroom, which we also shared, was more than adequate with a wonderful shower. It also helped that René was extremely neat and didn't snore.

What I didn't know, since it hadn't been mentioned at my interview, was that Mrs. Phipps was celebrating her seventieth birthday in July and had invited *scores* of friends and relations to join the festivities at luncheons and large dinner parties.

When Mrs. Phipps arrived several days later, she saw me for the first time and seemed about to faint. I had grown a beautiful, blond beard – the hirsute fad of the day. Mrs. Hedinger saw the beard when she interviewed me in New York but said nothing. I hadn't given it a second thought until I saw the reaction of my new employer.

However, appreciating the fact that finding another qualified Butler at that time in the season and especially in this location would be no easy task, Mrs. Phipps evidently decided that life with 'the bearded Butler' was something she could accept – for the time being at least.

But my beard soon became a game. She would say,

"Thomas, isn't your beard a little warm in this heat?" *or,*

"Thomas, how much extra time does it take you to trim your beard each morning?" *or,*

"Thomas, what possessed you to grow that beard? You have such a nice face." I invariably just smiled in response.

I realized that unless I acquiesced to her not-so-subtle requests to be clean-shaven the give-and-take would continue all summer. So as it happened one of the two greengrocers René (who didn't drive) and I visited almost daily – was next door to the only barber in town.

As René shopped, I entered the barbershop, plunked myself into a chair, and instructed the barber to "Shave off my beard." He did, and then asked if I wanted a haircut. I said, "Sure" and the result was my head now sported an extremely short haircut. I'll never forget the startled look on René's face when he saw me.

Later, Mrs. Phipps succinctly remarked that my new look was the 'lesser of two evils.'

A week later she asked me to drive her to Connecticut. She said the decision was mine since I was hired for the position of Butler, not chauffeur.

I decided to do it since I was anxious to get behind the wheel of her beautiful, four-door Mercedes-Benz. In any case, there weren't any guests in the house at the time so my Buttling skills were not required.

It seemed that one of her dear friends was celebrating his eightieth birthday with a dinner party at his Greenwich estate. The trip mandated an overnight stay since she planned to arrive for lunch, stay overnight and go back to Saratoga Springs the next morning.

I planned to take the New York State Thruway but Mrs. Phipps said she would rather take the Taconic State Parkway – a very beautiful, but notoriously difficult road to drive. It had been built as a WPA project in the 1930's and didn't have the safety factors of the more recent roads.

Mrs. Phipps opted to sit up front with me in order to enjoy the superb scenery. As I drove, we chatted. She asked me questions regarding my previous positions. She was eager to hear of my time at Mar-a-Lago. I also related the tale of Mr. Brian, the Gardners' sartorially-challenged

Butler and we laughed at his predicament. It was a pleasant drive and at one point she decided to address me as 'Tom,' rather than 'Thomas.'

As we drove, the weather changed (not an unusual summer happening in that mountainous region of upstate New York) – but just as we reached the summit of a very steep hill and began our descent – dark clouds filled the sky – lightning flashed and thunder boomed and a torrential rain began to fall. The rain was so heavy I couldn't see the road – even with the wipers at full speed.

And then it happened – the car began to hydroplane. It lost traction and was instantly transformed into an out-of-control – slipping – sliding – skidding down the hill – impossible to steer or brake, vehicle. With the realization that there was nothing to do, I took my foot off the gas pedal, hoping the car would slow down of its own accord, and all the while praying that we didn't skid off the road and down the embankment.

Mrs. Phipps wasn't wearing her seat belt and in an eerily calm voice, inquired,

"What should I do Tom?"

"Sit back, take a deep breath and close your eyes," I replied.

As you might imagine the next few seconds seemed like forever. At one point, the wheels on the passenger-side left the paved road and found footing in the rough gravel just off the highway. The noise was deafening. I was struggling so intensely to hold the steering wheel straight that my knuckles turned a bloodless white.

And suddenly, miraculously, I was in control again.

As we continued our two wheels on and two wheels off the paved road descent, I knew things would be all right. When at last we reached the bottom of the hill, I braked cautiously and brought the Mercedes to a stop. Only then did we turn to each other and share a smile of relief. I remember her simple comment,

"Well done, Tom. Thank you."

"You're very welcome, Mrs. Phipps."

We arrived in Greenwich in time for Mrs. Phipps to join the birthday boy and his guests for lunch. I'm sure that her vivid recounting of our harrowing adventure enthralled everyone there.

I checked into a nearby motel, took a long, hot shower and called a friend in Pound Ridge who unfortunately already had dinner plans. There's nothing like a brush with death to whet your appetite for life, so dined alone in one of Greenwich's finer restaurants, and slept like a baby that night.

I picked up Mrs. Phipps at nine-thirty the next morning and we drove back to Saratoga. We used the Thruway this time. Mrs. Phipps sat in the back and slept most of the way.

Mrs. Phipps was born Lillian Stokes Bostwick in New York City in 1906. She was the daughter of Mary Stokes and Albert Bostwick. Her paternal grandfather Jabez Bostwick was, along with John D. Rockefeller, William Rockefeller, Henry Flagler and Samuel Andrews, one of the founding partners of the Standard Oil Company. Her father Albert was a horseman and a polo player whose influence on Lillian and her brothers, Pete, Dunbar and Albert Jr., led to their interest and involvement in the sport of horse racing.

Lillian married South Carolinian, Robert V. McKim in 1928. The couple had three daughters, one of whom became the Palm Beach fashion designer, Lilly Pulitzer. In the 1930s Lillian, Pete and Dunbar built Bostwick Field in Old Westbury, Long Island where they hosted international polo matches.

The McKims eventually divorced. In 1937 she married the champion tennis player, thoroughbred horse breeder and stable owner, Ogden Phipps. They had two children, Ogden Mills (Dinny) and Cynthia. A prominent figure during the Saratoga Springs summer racing season for years, Mrs. Phipps owned and raced steeplechase horses that competed in her colors – gold silks with purple sleeves and cap. (A steeplechase is a fixed distance race with various jumping obstacles such as fences and water-filled ditches.)

Ogden Phipps was born in 1908 in New York City to Gladys Livingston Mills and Henry Carnegie Phipps. He attended Harvard College and rose to the rank of Commander in the U.S. Navy in World War II.

His paternal grandfather, Henry Phipps was one of Andrew Carnegie's partners in the Carnegie Steel Company. Carnegie owned fifty-five percent, Henry Clay Frick and Mr. Phipps owned eleven percent each. In 1901 Carnegie sold the company to J.P. Morgan who later founded U.S. Steel. Mr. Phipps and Mr. Frick netted fifty million dollars each.

In 1907 Phipps established the Bessemer Trust Company to manage his family's assets. The name honors Henry Bessemer, the English inventor of a process for making inexpensive steel – an essential factor in the success of Carnegie Steel.

Ogden's mother, Gladys Mills Phipps, launched the Phipps thoroughbred-racing dynasty in 1926 when she and her brother Ogden Mills established the well-known Wheatley Racing Stable at Claiborne Farm near Paris, Kentucky. The New York Times dubbed her 'First Lady of the Turf.'

(Thoroughbred, or flat racing, is the best-known form of horse racing. The horses compete over a fixed distance. The track is as a rule, oval and its surface can be earth, turf, or synthetic. There are no obstacles to jump. The race tests only the speed and stamina of the animals.)

In 1932 Ogden began a career in investment banking at Charles D. Barney & Co. He divorced his first wife Ruth Pruyn Phipps in 1935. In 1936 Ruth married Ogden's close friend, Marshall Field III. In 1937 Ogden became a partner at Smith, Barney & Co. and married Lillian Bostwick.

After forty years together the Phipps's, though not divorced, led separate lives. In 1973 Mr. Phipps commissioned a magnificent, one-hundred-eight-foot, four-stateroom cruiser from Burger Boats of Manitowoc, Wisconsin. He named the yacht for his favorite thoroughbred, *Buckpasser,* the 1966 'Horse of the Year.' Buckpasser was regarded as the best horse to wear the famed black silks and cherry-red cap of the Phipps stable.

Mr. Phipps spent most of the year on the yacht. He was scheduled to arrive in Saratoga for the running of the Travers Stakes on the last Saturday in August.

Several days after our harrowing trip to Greenwich the houseguests began to arrive for the birthday celebration. Among them were Robert Denning and Vincent Fourcade who occupied Mr. Phipps's former bedroom suite on the second floor.

The remaining houseguest roster was Mrs. Phipps's brother Dunbar and his wife, and Mrs. Phipps's daughter Lilly McKim Rousseau (formerly Lilly Pulitzer) and her husband. Her teenage grandchildren were quartered in the vacant staff bedrooms in the attic. Adding to this list was her close friend, Mrs. Garrison who flew in from Gardiner's Island on her private jet. The remaining family members were lodged in nearby hotels and guest-houses. Ogden Phipps did not attend the birthday celebration.

The workload was staggering. For four consecutive days we began work at six-thirty in the morning and we never retired before midnight. There were breakfasts for the houseguests and the children, luncheons, cocktail hours and formal dinner parties for up to sixteen people.

And each afternoon several children of the players at the Saratoga Springs Performing Arts Center would arrive to swim in the pool and were closely monitored for safety reasons.

For the first of several scheduled birthday dinners, the table held a fortune in antique china, silver, crystal, fine linens and exquisite flowers. René, the chef, prepared a superb French meal – a first course of braised leek followed by a *blanquette-de-veau* with white rice, accompanied by a dry Rosé from Provence. Everything went smoothly until the first course finished.

It was then that Jenny – the Skidmore College temporary parlor-maid, began moving from guest to guest, picking up the soiled dishes and then stacking them on her arm as if she was in a greasy spoon. She had once been a part-time waitress for an in-town diner and had no idea how to serve a formal dinner.

Glancing at Mrs. Phipps, I could see she was silently fuming. I whispered to Jenny as she passed me by,

"Jenny clear just one dish at a time." She looked up at me and asked, "Why?"

"Just do it!" I answered angrily, through clenched teeth. For the rest of the service I was on pins and needles hoping that nothing else would go wrong. Nothing did.

When the dinner service ended it was too late for Jenny to bicycle back to her Skidmore dormitory so I drove her there in the estate wagon. Though exhausted, I was on my way to relax in the local 'in' disco. On the way I volunteered to instruct her in the art of waiting table. Jenny was not in the least bit interested but I insisted and the next morning – I taught her the basics.

By the third day of this marathon performance, the entire staff was dog-tired. The ratio of staff to guests was totally out of proportion. René was at the brink of collapse as was I. Another formal dinner party for ten was scheduled that evening,. René had given me a copy of the menu so I could determine the necessary quantity and type of china, crystal, flatware and serving silver for the meal. A fresh and more elaborate flower arrangement arrived in the late afternoon and I readied the table making sure that all the necessary items were accurately placed and spotless. I cast one final glance around the room to be sure nothing had been overlooked and went to my room for a quick nap.

When the five o'clock staff dinner finished, I changed into my Butler's livery and set up the cocktail hour in the library. When the guests arrived at seven, I made all their drinks and Jenny passed trays of hors-d'oeuvres.

Then I checked with René and determined that dinner was ready, made sure that Jenny was standing by, and then entered the dining room and lit all the candles while Jenny poured the ice water. Finally, I notified Mrs. Phipps that everything was synchronized and she could announce dinner at her pleasure.

About fifteen minutes later Mrs. Phipps and her guests entered the dining room. As I seated Mrs. Phipps she turned around and, looking up at me, asked in a hoarse whisper,

"Tom, where is my napkin?" I glanced down at her place plate and then around the table. No napkins! I had forgotten the napkins!

My next move was pure 'Livingston' Without missing a beat I assessed the situation and rushed to the pantry. I spotted the ten neatly-folded napkins tucked in a corner. I found a silver serving tray and quickly arranged them in a clever rosette. Back in the dining room I presented Mrs. Phipps her napkin first and, gliding silently around the table offered the napkins – first to the ladies and then to the gentlemen. No one seemed to have noticed my 'exhaustion-provoked' gaff.

And so was born an additional dinner course that would be incorporated into all the future Saratoga formal dinners, 'The Serving of the Napkins.' (Just kidding!)

The next evening was Mrs. Phipps' actual birthday and the dinner party for sixteen went off perfectly.

Two days later the last of the houseguests were scheduled to depart. Messrs. Denning and Fourcade had driven up in their own car, which they always left in the driveway. Mrs. Garrison had arranged for her pilot to arrive before noon and fly her back to Gardiner's Island.

At around ten Mrs. Phipps and Mrs. Garrison had finished their breakfasts and were having coffee in the dining room. Denning and Fourcade were still upstairs in their bedroom and had not yet called for their breakfasts.

Mrs. Phipps called me to the dining room and informed me that Jenny had brought down Mrs. Garrison's bags and left them on the front porch. She asked me to put them in the trunk of Denning and Fourcade's car since it was the vehicle that would take Mrs. Garrison to the airport. I assumed that I would drive her there as both men were still asleep.

The bags were on the front porch and car's trunk was open. Without a second thought, I put the bags in the trunk and closed the hatch. The car, at that time, was facing the back of the house so I decided to turn it around in order to facilitate an easier exit. But when I got inside, I saw that the ignition key was missing.

I looked in the glove compartment, under the floor mat, even behind the sun visor – no key. I went back inside the house and checked the tray on the hall table – no key.

Then the phone rang. It was Mrs. Garrison's pilot. Her plane had landed and had a ten forty-five window for departure. I told Mrs. Phipps that I would have to wake Denning and Fourcade to get their car key. She agreed. I went to their door and knocked. They informed me, through the closed door that the key should be in the car as that's where they left it when they came back the previous afternoon's outing.

Moments later they arrived in their in robes and slippers and joined the group out on the front porch, now totaling five 'mindset change' Mrs. Phipps, Mrs. Garrison, the two designers and me. On seeing their car – one of them shrieked,

"Where are our antiques?"

It seemed the pair had gone to the antique shops in the area and made several purchases the previous day. Upon their return and not wishing to unload their treasures, they simply left them, not only in plain view on the back seat of the car but also in the trunk. And they left their key in the ignition. After all, the car was *on the property*. No one would dare touch it.

But during the night thieves had not only made off with their antiques but also, as I learned later, tossed the ignition key into the bushes.

So there we stood – Mrs. Phipps, the two slightly hysterical interior designers, Mrs. Garrison with her luggage securely locked in the trunk and no key to unlock it and her plane ready to take off – and I.

Suddenly Mrs. Phipps, her face livid with rage turned to me and said in a voice heard by one and all,

"Tom! How could you have been so *STUPID* as to put the bags in the trunk without making sure you had the key to the car?"

I was incensed as well, but I didn't show it. I would not accept being dressed down for that situation. For the better part of a month and a half I had not only worked harder and longer than I ever had before, but also, volunteered to do extra services, trained an unwilling young girl in the art of waiting table, shaved off my beard and – most significantly – *saved her life* on the Taconic Parkway.

A sense of great calm swept over me – I had finally made the decision I had been pondering for weeks.

I said not a word. I simply waited until she, having run out of venom, and perhaps realizing that she had gone too far, sputtered to a stop. But it was far too late.

Looking her straight in the eye, I simply said,

"Goodbye, Mrs. Phipps."

"What?" she said, "What did you say?"

"I said, Goodbye, Mrs. Phipps."

And as I walked away she threatened loudly – for one and all to hear,

"You can't leave! If you do, I won't give you a Reference!"

I turned around and facing both Mrs. Phipps and the entire group, I said,

"Mrs. Phipps, why do you think I need or want *your* Reference?"

Back in New York ten days later my mother told me that Mrs. Levy had called. I returned her call and related the Phipps saga. She said, "One of her horses must have lost that week." We both laughed.

Then she mentioned that she had run into Mrs. Phipps at the Keystone Racetrack in Bucks County, Pennsylvania and somehow their conversation turned to me. She said that Mrs. Phipps told her that I was, "a very accommodating, bright, trustworthy and resourceful young man" and in retrospect was sorry she lost her composure and turned on me because the problem had been easily solved by sending Mrs. Garrison to the airport in a taxi and a bit later, finding the ignition key in the bushes. It was then that Mrs. Levy inquired if I could come to Philadelphia as soon as possible since her new Butler was on the verge of leaving. (From boredom, I presumed.)

I hadn't thought of rejoining the Levys since I was planning an open-ended trip to Paris with an antiques dealer friend of mine. He had volunteered to take me on as an assistant and teach me the antiques business – my potential new career.

I told Mrs. Levy my new plan. She couldn't have been more gracious and understanding and wished me good luck and a bright and happy future.

Thank you, Estée Lauder.

(Addendum: We stayed in Paris four years. We founded an export business there and supplied several major American galleries in New York and elsewhere with fine French antiques. In 1980 we decided that the time had come to return home and open our own gallery. I was at that time a full partner in the business. The Gallery was on Madison Avenue between East 65th and East 66th Streets. Hildegarde Schine lived around the corner. Shortly after our opening she arrived at the Gallery with a friend and insisted on buying something to wish me luck.)

(A thought in closing: The purpose of this work was my desire to share with you the unique events that I, a young, middle class American male, was fortunate to experience. It all began with my choice of a rather unusual summer job. The unexpected variety my employers, my fellow staff members and the locations, all added to the flow and texture of the story. I honestly believe

what I found in each household was a unique insight as to what it meant (and means) to be rich in America, then and now.)

Thank you for sharing my journey.

Made in the USA
Coppell, TX
20 May 2024

32608730R00106